LIVING LITURGY™

Prayer Book for Extraordinary Ministers of Holy Communion

Year B • 2027

Katharine E. Harmon
Orin E. Johnson
Rámond Mitchell
Matthew Sherman

LITURGICAL PRESS
Collegeville, Minnesota

litpress.org

Cover design by Monica Bokinskie. Art by Br. Martin Erspamer, OSB, a monk of Saint Meinrad Archabbey, Indiana.

Nihil Obstat: Rev. Robert C. Harren, J.C.L., *Censor Librorum*
Imprimatur: ✠ Most Rev. Patrick M. Neary, C.S.C., Bishop of St. Cloud, May 12, 2026

ISSN 1933-3129

ISBN 979-8-4008-0214-0

Presented to

in grateful appreciation
for ministering as an
Extraordinary Minister
of
Holy Communion

(date)

USING THIS RESOURCE

Extraordinary typically refers to outstanding or exceptional. But extraordinary ministers of Holy Communion are "extra"ordinary in the sense of "in addition to" the ordinary (as well as being outstanding and exceptional!). Ordinary ministers of Holy Communion are the ordained and those properly installed as acolytes, usually seminarians. In parishes today there are simply not enough "ordinary" ministers of Holy Communion, so we call forth additional ministers, referred to as "extraordinary." Imagine how long the distribution of Communion would take if only the ordained or seminarians were those who distributed! It is not only because of need, however, that we have extraordinary ministers of Holy Communion. It is also by virtue of one's baptism. We parishioners are grateful that so many baptized Christians respond to the call to serve as extraordinary ministers of Holy Communion. In so doing we are reminded that we are all holy, and we are all called to ministry by virtue of our Christian baptism.

A Ministry of Prayer

Every ministry of the church requires regular prayer, reflection, reading, and thoughtfulness. For extraordinary ministers of Holy Communion, who enter regularly into the graced encounter between communicant and the living Christ, it is important to cultivate a prayer practice that can open their own eyes and hearts to the presence of Christ. This book is intended to sustain and support ministers by providing prayers and reflection for each Sunday and for certain solemnities.

Holy Communion for the Homebound and Sick

In the New Testament Letter of James we learn about the concern and care that the early Christians had for those members of their community who were sick. Such care and concern was a hallmark of Jesus's own ministry, and it has been a Christian charism ever since. Each week there are parishioners who are not able to join us for the liturgy, and so the Eucharist is brought to them as a sign of our unity.

Extraordinary ministers of Holy Communion are often those who perform this ministry, and, in so doing, they extend the parish's reach to so many more fellow parishioners. This book is intended to be a resource for them as well.

Adapting This Resource for Holy Communion for the Homebound and Sick

The Communion rite (Ordinary Rite of Communion of the Sick) is provided in the front of this book. Those who are extraordinary ministers of Holy Communion have undoubtedly been made familiar with this rite as part of their preparation. This book may be adapted for use with the rite, by sharing the gospel reflection, the prayers, or even the reflection question, so that the visit becomes a true ministry. It is to be remembered that ministers are not mere functionaries. As such, extraordinary ministers of Holy Communion bring not only the presence of Christ in the eucharistic species, but the presence of Christ in their very person by virtue of their baptism. So this book has been designed with that in mind, and it can be used to assist with making this a meaningful encounter and ministry.

Ongoing Formation in Ministry

Dioceses and parishes have slightly different preparation requirements for those who would be extraordinary ministers of Holy Communion, but most involve both initial preparation as well as ongoing formation. We know that it is not enough to simply attend a training event and never look back. Liturgical ministers must continue to grow in their understanding of their ministry, and of the liturgy itself. Indeed, like all who participate in the liturgy, liturgical ministers grow in discipleship and the paschal mystery of Jesus Christ *through* their liturgical ministry. As Pope Francis reminded us in his apostolic letter on liturgical formation, in the liturgy the paschal mystery is "rendered present and active by means of signs addressed to the senses (water, oil, bread, wine, gestures, words), so that the Spirit, plunging us into the paschal mystery, might transform every dimension of our life, conforming us more and more to Christ" (*Desiderio desideravi* 21).

In this regard, *Living Liturgy™ Prayer Book for Extraordinary Ministers of Holy Communion* is the ideal prayer complement to *Living Liturgy™: Spirituality, Celebration, and Catechesis for Sundays and Solemnities*, which provides transformative spiritual formation and liturgical catechesis for all liturgical ministers and the entire parish community. Whether used in tandem with *Living Liturgy™*, or on its own, the particular value of *Living Liturgy™ Prayer Book* is to cultivate in those who use it a prayerful spirit and a deeper sense of the real presence of Christ in the Eucharist.

ADMINISTRATION OF COMMUNION TO THE SICK BY AN EXTRAORDINARY MINISTER

When the Most Holy Eucharist is brought to the sick by an acolyte or an extraordinary minister of Holy Communion deputed in accordance with the norm of law, the rites to be observed are found in chapter two of *Holy Communion and Worship of the Eucharistic Mystery outside Mass*. "The Ordinary Rite of Communion of the Sick," provided below, is an extract of this ritual book, which also includes "A Shorter Rite of Communion of the Sick" and "Viaticum" as administered by an extraordinary minister. Please see *Communion of the Sick*, published by Liturgical Press, for all three rites. The Pastoral Notes at the end offer important reminders from the ritual book.

THE ORDINARY RITE OF COMMUNION OF THE SICK

THE INTRODUCTORY RITES

Wearing vestments appropriate for this ministry, after approaching the sick person, the minister warmly greets them and the others present, using, if appropriate, the greeting:

Peace to this house and all here.

Other words from Sacred Scripture, with which the faithful are customarily greeted, may also be used. Then, after placing the Sacrament on a table, the minister and all present adore it.

The minister invites the sick person and others present to take part in the Penitential Act:

Brethren (Brothers and sisters), let us acknowledge our sins, and so prepare ourselves to participate in this sacred celebration.

A brief pause for silence follows. Then all recite together the I confess:

I confess to almighty God
and to you, my brothers and sisters,
that I have greatly sinned,
in my thoughts and in my words,
in what I have done and in what I have failed to do,

And, striking their breast, they say:

through my fault, through my fault,
through my most grievous fault;

Then they continue:

therefore I ask blessed Mary ever-Virgin,
all the Angels and Saints,
and you, my brothers and sisters,
to pray for me to the Lord our God.

Or after a brief pause of silence, the minister, or one of those present, then says the following or other invocations:

You gained salvation for us by your Paschal Mystery: Lord, have mercy.

All: Lord, have mercy.

You never cease to renew among us the wonders of your Passion: Christ, have mercy.

All: Christ, have mercy.

You make us sharers in your Paschal Sacrifice through the reception of your Body: Lord, have mercy.

All: Lord, have mercy.

The minister concludes:

**May almighty God have mercy on us,
forgive us our sins,
and bring us to everlasting life.**

All reply: Amen.

THE SHORTER READING OF THE WORD OF GOD

It is very appropriate that one of those present or the minister read a brief text of Sacred Scripture. Readings may also be drawn from the Mass of the day or of the nearest Sunday, especially for ongoing ministry to sick and homebound persons.

John 6:54-58

**Whoever eats my Flesh and drinks my Blood
has eternal life,
and I will raise him on the last day.
For my Flesh is true food,
and my Blood is true drink.
Whoever eats my Flesh and drinks my Blood
remains in me and I in him.
Just as the living Father sent me**

and I have life because of the Father,
so also the one who feeds on me
will have life because of me.
This is the bread that came down from heaven.
Unlike your ancestors who ate and still died,
whoever eats this bread will live forever.

John 14:6

I am the way and the truth and the life.
No one comes to the Father except through me.

John 14:27

Peace I leave with you; my peace I give to you.
Not as the world gives do I give it to you.
Do not let your hearts be troubled or afraid.

John 15:5

I am the vine, you are the branches.
Whoever remains in me and I in him will bear much fruit,
because without me you can do nothing.

1 John 4:16

We have come to know and to believe in the love God has for us.
God is love, and whoever remains in love
remains in God and God in him.

Another appropriate text may also be chosen from those found in *Holy Communion and Worship of the Eucharistic Mystery outside Mass, The Order of the Anointing of the Sick and of their Pastoral Care,* or the *Lectionary for Mass.*

HOLY COMMUNION

Then the minister introduces the Lord's Prayer in these or similar words:

Now let us together call upon God,
as our Lord Jesus Christ taught us to pray:

And all together continue:

Our Father . . .

Then the minister shows the Most Blessed Sacrament, saying:

Behold the Lamb of God,
behold him who takes away the sins of the world.
Blessed are those called to the supper of the Lamb.

The sick person and any others who will receive Communion say once:

Lord, I am not worthy
that you should enter under my roof,
but only say the word
and my soul shall be healed.

The minister approaches the sick person, and showing them the Sacrament, says:

The Body of Christ (or: **The Blood of Christ**).

The sick person replies:

Amen.

And receives Holy Communion.

Those present who wish to receive Communion receive the Sacrament in the usual way.

When the distribution of Communion is complete, the minister carries out the purification as usual. Then, if appropriate, a sacred silence may be observed for a while.

The minister says the concluding prayer. One of the following may be used:

Let us pray.

**O Lord, holy Father, almighty and eternal God,
with faith we entreat you
that the most holy Body (most holy Blood)
of our Lord Jesus Christ your Son
may benefit our brother (sister) who receives it
as an everlasting remedy
for both body and soul.
Through Christ our Lord.**

Or:

**O God, who have accomplished the work of human redemption
through the Paschal Mystery of your Only Begotten Son,
graciously grant that we, who confidently proclaim,
under sacramental signs, the Death and Resurrection of Christ,
may experience continued increase of your saving grace.
Through Christ our Lord.**

Or:

May sharing at the heavenly table
sanctify us, Lord, we pray,
so that through the Body and Blood of Christ
the whole family of believers may be bound together.
Through Christ our Lord.

Or:

Pour on us, O Lord, the Spirit of your love,
and in your kindness
make those you have nourished
by this one heavenly Bread
one in mind and heart.
Through Christ our Lord.

All reply: Amen.

THE CONCLUDING RITES

Then the minister, while invoking God's blessing and signing himself (herself), says:

May the Lord bless us,
protect us from all evil
and lead us to everlasting life.

All reply: Amen.

Or:

May the almighty and merciful Lord bless us and keep us,
the Father, and the Son, and the Holy Spirit.

All reply: Amen.

PASTORAL NOTES

This rite is for use by an Extraordinary Minister of Holy Communion and is taken from *Holy Communion and Worship of the Eucharistic Mystery outside Mass*. The numbered citations below come from that book. A Priest or Deacon administers Holy Communion and Viaticum to the sick according to the rites in *The Order of the Anointing of the Sick and of their Pastoral Care* (no. 55).

Pastors of souls should take care that the sick and aged, even if not gravely sick or in imminent danger of death, should be given the opportunity to receive the Eucharist frequently, even, insofar as possible, daily, especially during Easter Time (no. 14).

The faithful are to be carefully taught that, even when they receive Communion outside the celebration of Mass, they are intimately united with the Sacrifice which perpetuates the Sacrifice of the Cross, and they are participants in that sacred banquet in which, "by Communion in the Body and Blood of the Lord, the People of God participates in the blessings of the Paschal Sacrifice, renews the New Covenant made once by God with men in the Blood of Christ, and in faith and hope prefigures and anticipates the eschatological banquet in the Kingdom of the Father, proclaiming the Death of the Lord until he comes" (no. 15).

Holy Communion may be given outside Mass on any day and at any time of the day . . . on Holy Saturday, Holy Communion may be given only as Viaticum" (no. 16).

It is first of all for the Priest or Deacon to administer Holy Communion to the faithful who ask for it. It is in every way proper, therefore, that they should give part of their time to the performance of this ministry, according to the needs of the faithful. Moreover, it is for a duly instituted acolyte, as an extraordinary minister, to give Holy Communion whenever there is no Priest or Deacon, either because of sickness, old age, or because they are prevented by pastoral duties or the number of faithful coming to the holy table is so great that the celebration of the Mass or other sacred celebration may be greatly prolonged. The local Ordinary may give the faculty of distributing Holy Communion to other extraordinary ministers, whenever it may seem necessary for the pastoral benefit of the faithful, and a Priest or Deacon or acolyte is not available (no. 17).

The minister of Holy Communion, if he is a Priest or Deacon, should be vested in an alb, or a surplice over a cassock, and should wear a stole. Other ministers should wear either the liturgical vesture traditional in their region or vesture which is not unsuitable for this ministry and is approved by the Ordinary. The Eucharist for administering Communion outside the church should be carried in a pyx or other closed vessel, with such coverings and in such a manner as is appropriate to the place (no. 20).

It is permitted to administer the Eucharist under the species of wine alone to those who are unable to receive it under the species of bread. The Blood of the Lord must be carried to the sick person in a vessel so closed as to avoid completely any danger of spillage. In administering the Sacrament, however, the more appropriate manner should be chosen, in each case, from those proposed for distributing Communion under both kinds. When Communion is completed, if any of the Most Precious Blood remains, it should be consumed by the minister, who should also take care of the necessary purifications (no. 55).

The Eucharist, which continuously represents the Paschal Mystery of Christ in the midst of humanity, is the fount of all grace and of the remission of sins. Nevertheless, those who intend to receive the Body of the Lord, should come to it with clean consciences and properly disposed souls, so that they may harvest the fruits of the paschal Sacrament . . . If there is a serious reason and no opportunity for confession, they should make an act of perfect contrition with the intention of confessing individually, as soon as possible, the mortal sins that they cannot confess at present. It is desirable that those who are accustomed to communicate daily or quite often go to the Sacrament of Penance at regular intervals, depending on their circumstances. Moreover, the faithful should look on the Eucharist as an antidote that frees them from daily faults and preserves them from mortal sins; in addition, they should understand the right way to use the penitential parts of the liturgy, especially of the Mass (no. 23).

Communicants should not receive the Sacrament unless they have fasted for at least one hour from food and drink, with the sole exceptions of water and medicine. The elderly and those suffering from any kind of infirmity, as well as those who take care of such persons, may receive the Most Holy Eucharist even if they have consumed something within the hour before (no. 24).

In order that they may more easily continue the act of thanksgiving which is offered to God in a splendid way in the Mass, it is recommended that all who have been refreshed in Holy Communion should continue in prayer for a certain period of time (no. 25).

Prayer

God of all seasons, you call us to watch and wait amid the hurry of life. Help us to find quiet space to notice your presence not far away but here and now in the ordinary moments you make holy each day. **Amen.**

Gospel **Mark 13:33-37**

Jesus said to his disciples: "Be watchful! Be alert! You do not know when the time will come. It is like a man traveling abroad. He leaves home and places his servants in charge, each with his own work, and orders the gatekeeper to be on the watch. Watch, therefore; you do not know when the lord of the house is coming, whether in the evening, or at midnight, or at cockcrow, or in the morning. May he not come suddenly and find you sleeping. What I say to you, I say to all: 'Watch!'"

Brief Silence

For Reflection

The gospel that begins our new liturgical year admonishes us, the faithful, to watch and be alert. Why? Because, simply, we do not know. In this pericope what is unknown is "when the lord of the house is coming." But for each of us today, this gospel calls us to embrace the unknown, as another expression goes, and to participate, actively, in our lives of faith instead of anticipating. So in fact, the gospel is calling us, really, to not know—and to be okay with not knowing.

✦ Where, in your life, are you "asleep" to the needs of Christ and neighbor? How can you "wake up" to a new life of being attentive?

Brief Silence

Model Universal Prayer (Prayer of the Faithful)

Awake and ready to follow God's will, we turn to him with our prayers and petitions.

Response: Lord, hear our prayer.

For the church throughout the world: may the faithful await with joy the light of Christ and find freedom from the darkness of sin, loneliness, and suffering, we pray . . .

For greater peace in our hearts, in our communities, and among those who lead us: may we choose the mercy of Christ as we seek fellowship with our neighbors, we pray . . .

For hearts open to the suffering of those near us and those far away: may our watchfulness this Advent season open our hearts as well as our eyes, we pray . . .

For deepening of our attention and our focus: may we reject distractions and self-absorption to be truly present to those around us, we pray . . .

Almighty and ever-living God, you are the Alpha and the Omega. As we begin this Advent season, may we remember the wonder of your love through our mercy and compassion to all the world. We ask this through Christ our Lord. **Amen.**

Prayer

God of promise, you make straight the path for your coming. Help us clear away what weighs us down and open our hearts to your love. Give us patience to wait calmly and the joy to welcome you when you come in glory. **Amen.**

Gospel **Mark 1:1-8**

The beginning of the gospel of Jesus Christ the Son of God.

As it is written in Isaiah the prophet: / *Behold, I am sending my messenger ahead of you; / he will prepare your way. / A voice of one crying out in the desert: / "Prepare the way of the Lord, / make straight his paths."* / John the Baptist appeared in the desert proclaiming a baptism of repentance for the forgiveness of sins. People of the whole Judean countryside and all the inhabitants of Jerusalem were going out to him and were being baptized by him in the Jordan River as they acknowledged their sins. John was clothed in camel's hair, with a leather belt around his waist. He fed on locusts and wild honey. And this is what he proclaimed: "One mightier than I is coming after me. I am not worthy to stoop and loosen the thongs of his sandals. I have baptized you with water; he will baptize you with the Holy Spirit."

Brief Silence

For Reflection

In this gospel, John the Baptist teaches us by his words and example: how do we today prepare for the coming of the Lord? Christmas, we will recall, exists as a celebration of not only the eternal Word taking on human flesh, but of that second coming at the end of human time. Taking John's example, we might today choose to live more simply and to more freely share with those we encounter the way our lives have been impacted by our faith and our relationship with Jesus.

✦ What can you wash away from your life this Advent, in order to make way for Christ?

Brief Silence

Model Universal Prayer (Prayer of the Faithful)

In Christ, we seek to create a new heaven and a new earth by the power of our baptism. In the hope of this renewal, we bring our petitions to the Lord.

Response: Lord, hear our prayer.

For the church: that it may renew the earth by its faith-filled witness in the world, we pray . . .

For those who hold public office in this country and across the globe: that they may transform their civic systems to best serve God's people, we pray . . .

For those who are in need of God's mercy: that all who yearn for mercy might find courage to reach out to the God of kindness and salvation, we pray . . .

For the members of this community: that we might seek God's way with repentance, striving, and joy, we pray . . .

God of mercy, your Son, Jesus Christ, came among us in order to renew both heaven and earth in the power of his light. Hear our petitions this day and, from your merciful heart, grant us the grace to receive your forgiveness, renewal, and strength. We ask this through Christ our Lord. **Amen.**

THE IMMACULATE CONCEPTION OF THE BLESSED VIRGIN MARY

Prayer

God, who preserved the Blessed Virgin Mary from all stain of sin, help us, called to serve your church, to follow her example of faithful obedience, that our words and actions may echo her yes and draw others ever closer to your saving grace. **Amen.**

Gospel **Luke 1:26-38**

The angel Gabriel was sent from God to a town of Galilee called Nazareth, to a virgin betrothed to a man named Joseph, of the house of David, and the virgin's name was Mary. And coming to her, he said, "Hail, full of grace! The Lord is with you." But she was greatly troubled at what was said and pondered what sort of greeting this might be. Then the angel said to her, "Do not be afraid, Mary, for you have found favor with God. Behold, you will conceive in your womb and bear a son, and you shall name him Jesus. He will be great and will be called Son of the Most High, and the Lord God will give him the throne of David his father, and he will rule over the house of Jacob forever, and of his Kingdom there will be no end." But Mary said to the angel, "How can this be, since I have no relations with a man?" And the angel said to her in reply, "The Holy Spirit will come upon you, and the power of the Most High will overshadow you. Therefore the child to be born will be called holy, the Son of God. And behold, Elizabeth, your relative, has also conceived a son in her old age, and this is the sixth month for her who was called barren; for nothing will be impossible for God." Mary said, "Behold, I am the handmaid of the Lord. May it be done to me according to your word." Then the angel departed from her.

Brief Silence

For Reflection

God speaks to us as did the angel to Mary in this gospel: "Do not be afraid." Why might we be afraid? Because so often God's call to us is shrouded in the unknown. Have you ever had that itch, that mysterious prod in your side that makes you feel called to something else—but you can't quite put your finger on it? And yet each time it's been God, calling not to personal desires, knowledge, or power but to faith in the divine mystery and mission. "How can this be?" indeed.

✦ Can you recall a time when you have been afraid of something new in your life, a time when you were changed by that newness?

Brief Silence

Model Universal Prayer (Prayer of the Faithful)

Like our mother, Mary, the Lord invites us to come to him with trust and hope. We turn to him with our prayers and petitions.

Response: Lord, hear our prayer.

For Pope N.: may he be filled with the wisdom of the Spirit in leading the faithful and promoting peace in the world, we pray . . .

For the lawmakers around the world: may they boldly defend vulnerable people from conception to natural death, we pray . . .

For all who hope for safety and stability in their lives: may they be freed from fear, escape violence, and find refuge, we pray . . .

For friends and loved ones suffering from anxiety, depression, and mental illness: may they find comfort, and may we support them with patience, we pray . . .

Lord our God, your servant Mary is mother of the church and mother of our Lord. Grant us courage to have faith as Mary did, and trust in your goodness. We ask this through Christ our Lord. **Amen**.

OUR LADY OF GUADALUPE

Prayer

God of compassion, through Mary's loving presence, you reached out to the humble and the hopeful.

Help us listen to her gentle call, to stand with the poor, and to live with courage and mercy every day.

Amen.

Gospel **Luke 1:26-38 (or Luke 1:39-47)**

The angel Gabriel was sent from God to a town of Galilee called Nazareth, to a virgin betrothed to a man named Joseph, of the house of David, and the virgin's name was Mary. And coming to her, he said, "Hail, full of grace! The Lord is with you." But she was greatly troubled at what was said and pondered what sort of greeting this might be. Then the angel said to her, "Do not be afraid, Mary, for you have found favor with God. Behold, you will conceive in your womb and bear a son, and you shall name him Jesus. He will be great and will be called Son of the Most High, and the Lord God will give him the throne of David his father, and he will rule over the house of Jacob forever, and of his Kingdom there will be no end." But Mary said to the angel, "How can this be, since I have no relations with a man?" And the angel said to her in reply, "The Holy Spirit will come upon you, and the power of the Most High will overshadow you. Therefore the child to be born will be called holy, the Son of God. And behold, Elizabeth, your relative, has also conccivcd a son in her old age, and this is the sixth month for her who was called barren; for nothing will be impossible for God." Mary said, "Behold, I am the handmaid of the Lord. May it be done to me according to your word." Then the angel departed from her.

Brief Silence

For Reflection

Very few of us will experience the divine presence the way that Mary did at the annunciation, nor experience Mary as Juan Diego did. Yet we are called to recognize that every human being is made in the image and likeness of God. Every human being, as Paul writes to the Corinthians, is "a temple of the holy Spirit" (1 Cor 6:19). In this way, the activity, the voice, and the love of God is closer to us than we may dare imagine—even within our own mortal shells.

✦ What are the ways you experience God's closeness?

Brief Silence

Model Universal Prayer (Prayer of the Faithful)

Joining Mary in unceasing prayer and hopefulness, we offer our petitions.

Response: Lord, hear our prayer.

For the church: that it may shelter refugees, migrants, and all who must find safety this day, we pray . . .

For leaders of nations: that they might be especially mindful of the women who work each day to care for, feed, and protect their families, we pray . . .

For all Indigenous peoples: may they preserve and embrace their heritage while thriving in the present, we pray . . .

For the poor: especially those within our parish boundaries who live in the shadow of violence, we pray . . .

Lord God, you anoint the poor and the lowly as your beloved servants. Hear our prayers this day, and allow us to be filled with praise so that we might always rejoice in you. **Amen.**

Prayer

God of lasting joy, you sent John the Baptist to prepare us for the One who brings light. Gladden our hearts with your promise, so we may rejoice in hope, speak with honesty, and make a clear path for Christ, who is our joy and our peace. **Amen.**

Gospel **John 1:6-8, 19-28**

A man named John was sent from God. He came for testimony, to testify to the light, so that all might believe through him. He was not the light, but came to testify to the light.

And this is the testimony of John. When the Jews from Jerusalem sent priests and Levites to him to ask him, "Who are you?" he admitted and did not deny it, but admitted, "I am not the Christ." So they asked him, "What are you then? Are you Elijah?" And he said, "I am not." "Are you the Prophet?" He answered, "No." So they said to him, "Who are you, so we can give an answer to those who sent us? What do you have to say for yourself?" He said: / "I am *the voice of one crying out in the desert, / 'make straight the way of the Lord,'* / as Isaiah the prophet said." Some Pharisees were also sent. They asked him, "Why then do you baptize if you are not the Christ or Elijah or the Prophet?" John answered them, "I baptize with water; but there is one among you whom you do not recognize, the one who is coming after me, whose sandal strap I am not worthy to untie." This happened in Bethany across the Jordan, where John was baptizing.

Brief Silence

For Reflection

Christian paradox is perhaps best expressed in mystery—God's truth beyond all human understanding. In our Scriptures, these paradoxes abound: both greatness and lowliness, both strength and weakness, both light and darkness, both first and last, both humanity and divinity, both life and death, both one and many. In today's gospel, John the Baptist, while decidedly unjoyful, calls each of us to a most joyful pursuit: following the one true light in the darkness, which the darkness could not overcome.

✦ In what ways can you allow Christ to bring joy into your life more fully, so that your joy is a source of light and conversion for those around you?

Brief Silence

Model Universal Prayer (Prayer of the Faithful)

We come with hope before the Lord who offers us salvation, bringing our prayers for ourselves and all the world.

Response: Lord, hear our prayer.

For an increase in faith throughout the church, drawing the faithful to greater mercy and joy, we pray . . .

For courage among our leaders to remain steadfast in love for God and care for our neighbors, we pray . . .

For the poor, the hungry, and the brokenhearted among us and among the most vulnerable of the world, we pray . . .

For patience and peace with ourselves and with those who hate us, we pray . . .

God our Father, you have filled the hungry with good things and sent the rich away empty. Hear our prayers and petitions this day and fill us with your light so that we might go out to all the world to share the richness of Christ Jesus. We ask this through Christ our Lord. **Amen.**

Prayer

God of promise, you call us to watch and wait, preparing hearts to receive your Son. Fill us with the courage and trust of Mary, the joy of Elizabeth, and the patience to welcome Christ into our lives, that we may bear his light to the world. **Amen.**

Gospel **Luke 1:26-38**

The angel Gabriel was sent from God to a town of Galilee called Nazareth, to a virgin betrothed to a man named Joseph, of the house of David, and the virgin's name was Mary. And coming to her, he said, "Hail, full of grace! The Lord is with you." But she was greatly troubled at what was said and pondered what sort of greeting this might be. Then the angel said to her, "Do not be afraid, Mary, for you have found favor with God.

"Behold, you will conceive in your womb and bear a son, and you shall name him Jesus. He will be great and will be called Son of the Most High, and the Lord God will give him the throne of David his father, and he will rule over the house of Jacob forever, and of his kingdom there will be no end." But Mary said to the angel, "How can this be, since I have no relations with a man?" And the angel said to her in reply, "The Holy Spirit will come upon you, and the power of the Most High will overshadow you. Therefore the child to be born will be called holy, the Son of God. And behold, Elizabeth, your relative, has also conceived a son in her old age, and this is the sixth month for her who was called barren; for nothing will be impossible for God." Mary said, "Behold, I am the handmaid of the Lord. May it be done to me according to your word." Then the angel departed from her.

Brief Silence

For Reflection

It seems that even before Mary knew of her calling to become the mother of God incarnate that she must have already learned her faith well: from her parents, from rabbis and other holy men and women, and perhaps even from the ritual practices of her faith. Just as this gospel passage has been repetitive this Advent, the consistent presence of loved ones and faith-filled teachers, and the regular and unfailing practice of the rituals of her faith, surely embedded in Mary all that we know her to be.

✦ How can you be more willing to do God's will? What plans do you have that are impeding your ability to accept God's plans for you?

Brief Silence

Model Universal Prayer (Prayer of the Faithful)

By Mary's openness to God's will, we have found a place in our Lord's house forever. As his favored children, we now ask God for what we need.

Response: Lord, hear our prayer.

For the church, as it finishes its preparations for Christ's coming: may it never fail to find him in the poor and the afflicted, we pray . . .

For those in office: may they minister to those in their care with the generosity of God, and that they, too, may favor those on the margins, we pray . . .

For those who are homeless: may they, like the Holy Family, find God's care and protection in their hour of need, we pray . . .

For all gathered here: may the coming of the Lord be an experience of generosity and community, we pray . . .

God of power and compassion, your humble birth brought about a kingdom of true power and joy. Grant that we, like Mary, open ourselves to God's will. We ask this through Christ our Lord. **Amen.**

Prayer

Loving God, you sent your Son into the quiet of our world, wrapped in human frailty yet radiant with divine light. May his birth bring hope to the weary, joy to the sorrowful, and peace to hearts longing for your presence. Let us welcome him anew each day. **Amen.**

Gospel **Luke 2:1-14, Mass during the Night (or Matthew 1:1-25, Vigil Mass; or Luke 2:15-20, Mass at Dawn; or John 1:1-18, Mass during the Day)**

In those days a decree went out from Caesar Augustus that the whole world should be enrolled. This was the first enrollment, when Quirinius was governor of Syria. So all went to be enrolled, each to his own town. And Joseph too went up from Galilee from the town of Nazareth to Judea, to the city of David that is called Bethlehem, because he was of the house and family of David, to be enrolled with Mary, his betrothed, who was with child. While they were there, the time came for her to have her child, and she gave birth to her firstborn son. She wrapped him in swaddling clothes and laid him in a manger, because there was no room for them in the inn.

Now there were shepherds in that region living in the fields and keeping the night watch over their flock. The angel of the Lord appeared to them and the glory of the Lord shone around them, and they were struck with great fear. The angel said to them, "Do not be afraid; for behold, I proclaim to you good news of great joy that will be for all the people. For today in the city of David a savior has been born for you who is Christ and Lord. And this will be a sign for you: you will find an infant wrapped in swaddling clothes and lying in a manger." And suddenly there was a multitude of the heavenly host with the angel, praising God and saying: / "Glory to God in the highest / and on earth peace to those on whom his favor rests."

Brief Silence

For Reflection

Imagine Mary and Joseph, approaching their last chance for lodging that night, tired and worn, desperation perhaps obvious on their faces. Who would have noticed all this? The innkeeper, of course. We can further imagine the innkeeper having an almost unthinkable idea: "Well . . . I could offer you . . . what about the animal pen around the back?" It's not hard to imagine Mary and Joseph exuding immense gratefulness for such a strange offering. We often have more to give than we know.

✦ When have you been creative in helping others, or experienced the creative care of another?

Brief Silence

Model Universal Prayer (Prayer of the Faithful)

The Lord Jesus comes to us to fill the world with light. Let us who are called to be God's children offer our prayers and petitions for ourselves and all the world.

Response: Lord, hear our prayer.

For the church: may all the faithful be filled with grace and truth, and the courage to share Christ's light with all the world, we pray . . .

For all who believe in God: may those who share a love for God be blessed with peace, we pray . . .

For family members who are absent or estranged: may our prayers for their well-being bring them grace and guidance in the Spirit, we pray . . .

For greater joy: may we look at our loved ones and our lives and be reminded of God's abundant blessings, we pray . . .

O God, you sent your only Son into the world so that we might be saved through him. Hear our prayers, guide us in your truth, and allow us to be the light to all the nations that you have called your children to be. We ask this through Christ our Lord. **Amen.**

THE HOLY FAMILY OF JESUS, MARY, AND JOSEPH

Prayer

Father of all, you revealed the gift of family in Jesus, Mary, and Joseph. Bless our homes with patience, understanding, and love. Help us mirror their faithfulness in caring for one another, walking together in your ways, and honoring your presence in every moment of family life. **Amen.**

Gospel **Luke 2:22-40 (or Luke 2:22, 39-40)**

When the days were completed for their purification according to the law of Moses, they took him up to Jerusalem to present him to the Lord, just as it is written in the law of the Lord, *Every male that opens the womb shall be consecrated to the Lord,* and to offer the sacrifice of *a pair of turtledoves or two young pigeons,* in accordance with the dictate in the law of the Lord.

Now there was a man in Jerusalem whose name was Simeon. This man was righteous and devout, awaiting the consolation of Israel, and the Holy Spirit was upon him. It had been revealed to him by the Holy Spirit that he should not see death before he had seen the Christ of the Lord. He came in the Spirit into the temple; and when the parents brought in the child Jesus to perform the custom of the law in regard to him, he took him into his arms and blessed God, saying: / "Now, Master, you may let your servant go / in peace, according to your word, / for my eyes have seen your salvation, / which you prepared in sight of all the peoples, / a light for revelation to the Gentiles, / and glory for your people Israel." / The child's father and mother were amazed at what was said about him; and Simeon blessed them and said to Mary his mother, "Behold, this child is destined for the fall and rise of many in Israel, and to be a sign that will be contradicted—and you yourself a sword will pierce—so that the thoughts of many hearts may be revealed." There was also a prophetess, Anna, the daughter of Phanuel, of the tribe of Asher. She was advanced in years, having lived seven years with her husband after her marriage, and then as a widow until she was eighty-four. She never left the temple, but worshiped night and day with fasting and prayer. And coming forward at that very time, she gave thanks to God and spoke about the child to all who were awaiting the redemption of Jerusalem.

When they had fulfilled all the prescriptions of the law of the Lord, they returned to Galilee, to their own town of Nazareth. The child grew and became strong, filled with wisdom; and the favor of God was upon him.

Brief Silence

For Reflection

The elders of our faith communities have done and seen a lot of living. Along with holy wisdom, a long life grants to those blest with these years a certain perspective—sometimes optimistic, sometimes pessimistic, occasionally at the same time! Simeon and Anna speak about the child as the living embodiment of the hopes and expectations of all Jews awaiting the restoration of God's rule in Israel. The birth of Jesus brings these promises to fulfillment, but perhaps not in the earthly way that was hoped for and expected.

✦ Is your life full of conflict with family or friends? Do you know someone who struggles with such conflict? How can you help them? For what can you pray?

Brief Silence

THE HOLY FAMILY OF JESUS, MARY, AND JOSEPH

Model Universal Prayer (Prayer of the Faithful)

Turning to the Lord who cares for his people from age to age, we offer our prayers and petitions.
Response: Lord, hear our prayer.

For Christian families: may we choose to love one another and invite Christ into our homes with prayer . . .

For our grandparents, elders, and senior friends: may we seek their wisdom and honor their lives, we pray . . .

For children who do not have families to care for them: may they be received into loving homes and find comfort, we pray . . .

For greater confidence in the Spirit: may we have the faith of Simeon and the gratitude of Anna, we pray . . .

O God, you call us to love one another, beginning with those closest to us. Heal hearts that are wounded and revive spirits in need of joy, so that we might follow in the footsteps of the Holy Family. We ask this through Christ our Lord. **Amen.**

SOLEMNITY OF MARY, THE HOLY MOTHER OF GOD

Prayer

God of mercy, you chose Mary to bear your Son and bring salvation to the world. Fill us with wonder at your plan, courage to say yes to your call, and faith to follow where your Spirit leads, rejoicing in the gift of your Son. **Amen.**

Gospel **Luke 2:16-21**

The shepherds went in haste to Bethlehem and found Mary and Joseph, and the infant lying in the manger. When they saw this, they made known the message that had been told them about this child. All who heard it were amazed by what had been told them by the shepherds. And Mary kept all these things, reflecting on them in her heart. Then the shepherds returned, glorifying and praising God for all they had heard and seen, just as it had been told to them.

When eight days were completed for his circumcision, he was named Jesus, the name given him by the angel before he was conceived in the womb.

Brief Silence

For Reflection

In addition to celebrating the *Theotokos*, the "God-Bearer" today, January 1 is also the World Day of Peace. Mary herself is a shining example of peace, justice, and dignity. She is more than meek and mild, more than a lowly handmaid. Her *Magnificat* praises the God who casts down the mighty and raises the lowly. As we celebrate Mary the God-Bearer today, let us also recommit ourselves to the example given us by the Blessed Mother in prayer, in contemplation, and in action.

✦ How do you bring peace to others? What opportunities do you have to grow in peace?

Brief Silence

Model Universal Prayer (Prayer of the Faithful)

Reflecting on the words we have heard in the gospel, we offer our prayers and petitions.

Response: Lord, hear our prayer.

That we, the church, might hear the word of God this day and choose to act with new conviction to love, we pray . . .

That our nation might seek goodness, truth, and beauty in the governing of its people, we pray . . .

That all who are without food, shelter, or safety this day might be encouraged and find refuge, we pray . . .

That this new year might bring justice to all nations, hope to all peoples, and peace to all homes, we pray . . .

Lord God, your servant, Mary, heard your word and responded with faith. Fill our hearts with the same constancy and courage, that we might make your presence known to all the world. We ask this through Christ our Lord. **Amen.**

Prayer

God of light, you revealed your Son to the nations, guiding seekers to his presence. Open our eyes to see Christ in every neighbor, our hearts to follow where your star leads, and our lives to reflect his wisdom, justice, and love to the world. **Amen.**

Gospel **Matt 2:1-12**

When Jesus was born in Bethlehem of Judea, in the days of King Herod, behold, magi from the east arrived in Jerusalem, saying, "Where is the newborn king of the Jews? We saw his star at its rising and have come to do him homage." When King Herod heard this, he was greatly troubled, and all Jerusalem with him. Assembling all the chief priests and the scribes of the people, he inquired of them where the Christ was to be born. They said to him, "In Bethlehem of Judea, for thus it has been written through the prophet: / *And you, Bethlehem, land of Judah, / are by no means least among the rulers of Judah; / since from you shall come a ruler, / who is to shepherd my people Israel."* / Then Herod called the magi secretly and ascertained from them the time of the star's appearance. He sent them to Bethlehem and said, "Go and search diligently for the child. When you have found him, bring me word, that I too may go and do him homage." After their audience with the king they set out. And behold, the star that they had seen at its rising preceded them, until it came and stopped over the place where the child was. They were overjoyed at seeing the star, and on entering the house they saw the child with Mary his mother. They prostrated themselves and did him homage. Then they opened their treasures and offered him gifts of gold, frankincense, and myrrh. And having been warned in a dream not to return to Herod, they departed for their country by another way.

Brief Silence

For Reflection

Today we celebrate the visitation of the magi to the Christ Child. We hear very little in the gospel about the journey they must have taken: we know not from where they came and to where they returned, for instance. There is practical reason that "they departed for their country by another way": to avoid Herod. Yet there is also a theological reason: everyone in Scripture who encounters the divine has their life dramatically changed. One way is by upending, literally, their life's path.

✦ Like the magi, how in your life can you be willing to travel "by another way"? How might this way be both a choice for safety and a risk??

Brief Silence

Model Universal Prayer (Prayer of the Faithful)

Coming before the Lord, we offer our hearts as we pray for all those in need of light and life.

Response: Lord, hear our prayer.

That the church throughout the world, along with our Orthodox brothers and sisters, might find light, restoration, and peace in our time, we pray . . .

That leaders of nations may learn from the magi who listened to the words of God's angel and not the commands of earthly powers, we pray . . .

That children suffering from neglect, discrimination, and violence will find protection in their communities and from advocates throughout the world, we pray . . .

That the faithful gathered here might find renewed strength in their baptismal call to be priests, prophets, and kings, we pray . . .

O God, you sent your Son into the world so that all nations might come to know your glory. Hear our prayers this day and fill us with your grace so that we might fulfill our baptismal call to be your faithful daughters and sons. We ask this through Christ our Lord. **Amen.**

Prayer

God of glory, at the Jordan your Son was revealed as your beloved, and your Spirit rested upon him. Breathe that same Spirit into us, that we may rise to new life, embrace our calling, and live as your beloved children in service and love. **Amen.**

Gospel **Mark 1:7-11**

This is what John the Baptist proclaimed: "One mightier than I is coming after me. I am not worthy to stoop and loosen the thongs of his sandals. I have baptized you with water; he will baptize you with the Holy Spirit."

It happened in those days that Jesus came from Nazareth of Galilee and was baptized in the Jordan by John. On coming up out of the water he saw the heavens being torn open and the Spirit, like a dove, descending upon him. And a voice came from the heavens, "You are my beloved Son; with you I am well pleased."

Brief Silence

For Reflection

John the Baptist proclaims, "One mightier than I is coming after me." When Jesus arrives and steps into the water, something extraordinary happens. The sinless Son of God joins the line of sinners waiting to be baptized. The One who has no need of cleansing identifies himself completely with our human condition. This moment is not about Jesus's repentance, but about his solidarity—with the broken, the weary, and the searching. He sanctifies the waters by entering them, making them a channel of grace for all who will follow.

✦ Jesus reveals himself as the Son of God through his baptism. What does his baptism reveal to you that helps you to see him more accurately?

Brief Silence

Model Universal Prayer (Prayer of the Faithful)

The Lord has gone before us, leading us in faith and baptism. Trusting in his promises, we offer our prayers and petitions.

Response: Lord, hear our prayer.

For the church: may all the baptized grow in faith and determination to live in Christ Jesus, we pray . . .

For leaders of nations: may they protect all people of faith, refusing discrimination and ending persecution, we pray . . .

For the suffering and downhearted: may we remind them of the love of Christ Jesus with our encouragement, we pray . . .

For all those gathered here: may we remember our baptism each day, recalling that we have the gift of God's grace to be God's daughters and sons, we pray . . .

O God, you call us always to yourself. Hear our prayers this day, and fill our hearts with the desire to always walk in your ways and to remember that you love us. We ask this through Christ our Lord. **Amen.**

SECOND SUNDAY IN ORDINARY TIME

Prayer

God who calls, you invite us to follow your Son and share in his mission. Open our hearts to hear your voice, give us courage to answer without hesitation, and guide our steps, that we may witness your love and bring your light to those we meet. **Amen.**

Gospel **John 1:35-42**

John was standing with two of his disciples, and as he watched Jesus walk by, he said, "Behold, the Lamb of God." The two disciples heard what he said and followed Jesus. Jesus turned and saw them following him and said to them, "What are you looking for?" They said to him, "Rabbi"—which translated means Teacher—, "where are you staying?" He said to them, "Come, and you will see." So they went and saw where Jesus was staying, and they stayed with him that day. It was about four in the afternoon. Andrew, the brother of Simon Peter, was one of the two who heard John and followed Jesus. He first found his own brother Simon and told him, "We have found the Messiah"—which is translated Christ. Then he brought him to Jesus. Jesus looked at him and said, "You are Simon the son of John; you will be called Cephas"—which is translated Peter.

Brief Silence

For Reflection

In today's gospel, God's calls reach the ears, and indeed the very souls, of people not expecting it. We, too, are charged with calling and fashioning new disciples. How do we preach the good news to those who most need to hear it? Is that message of hope and salvation brought outside the church doors somehow? Are those fallen away from the faith invited to return? Our Jewish brothers and sisters name this act of welcoming the stranger *Hachnasat or'chim*. Might our church families also be blessed by our welcome?

✦ With whom in your life do you need to share Christ's invitation? What gifts do you have that would make you a more effective sharer of Christ's offer?

Brief Silence

Model Universal Prayer (Prayer of the Faithful)

We come before the Lord as his gathered assembly, praying for our community here and for all the world.

Response: Lord, hear our prayer.

For the young people of the church discerning their vocations as lay faithful, as priests, or as members of religious communities: may they hear the Spirit's prompting in the midst of pressures from the world, we pray . . .

For those in power who have not yet let the word of God pierce their hearts: may the Lord put a new song within their mouths, we pray . . .

For the sick and the suffering in mind, body, and spirit: may the grace of God break through barriers of hardship in their lives, we pray . . .

For all here struggling to find community and friendship: may they find courage to continue seeking relationships and may those around them recognize their need, we pray . . .

Lord God, sacrifice and offering you want not, but instead you desire hearts inscribed by your law. Hear our prayers as we offer them to you and fill us with your Spirit so that we might proclaim your justice to all the world. We ask this through Christ our Lord. **Amen.**

Prayer

Jesus, source of goodness, you call us to leave behind what binds us and follow you. Open our hearts to your teaching, strengthen our hands for service, and lead us to gather others into your mercy and love, that your kingdom may shine through our lives. **Amen.**

Gospel **Mark 1:14-20**

After John had been arrested, Jesus came to Galilee proclaiming the gospel of God: "This is the time of fulfillment. The kingdom of God is at hand. Repent, and believe in the gospel."

As he passed by the Sea of Galilee, he saw Simon and his brother Andrew casting their nets into the sea; they were fishermen. Jesus said to them, "Come after me, and I will make you fishers of men." Then they abandoned their nets and followed him. He walked along a little farther and saw James, the son of Zebedee, and his brother John. They too were in a boat mending their nets. Then he called them. So they left their father Zebedee in the boat along with the hired men and followed him.

Brief Silence

For Reflection

Jesus is always careful to meet each person where they are before inviting them into deeper holiness. Consider last week, where Jesus entered into some banter with Andrew and the other disciple and spent the whole afternoon with them. Consider that immediately upon meeting Simon, Jesus gives him a new name. Then consider today's gospel, where Jesus calls the fishermen to the ministry of evangelization and the saving of souls. Each apostle was met in a different way and brought into work of kingdom building on different terms.

✦ Like Jesus's first apostles, are you willing to drop what you are doing and follow with the same immediacy? If not, what's holding you back?

Brief Silence

Model Universal Prayer (Prayer of the Faithful)

The Lord calls us to repent and believe in the gospel, for the kingdom of God is at hand. Preparing for his coming, we offer our prayers and petitions for ourselves and for all the world.

Response: Lord, hear our prayer.

For those discerning full initiation into the Catholic Church: may the faithful encourage them with joy and hospitality, we pray . . .

For nations undergoing elections and changes in power: may peace reign, we pray . . .

For those who suffer from displacement due to climate change and social unrest: may they be led to resources that sustain their lives while they await safe return to their homelands, we pray . . .

For all gathered here today: may we remember the grace first received in our baptism to become sons and daughters of God, through Christ Jesus, sealed with the Holy Spirit, we pray . . .

O God, your Son called his disciples to himself, offering them mercy and the forgiveness of their sins. May we remain steadfast in following his call, courageous in our rejection of sin, and constant in inviting all the world to love you more. We ask this through Christ our Lord. **Amen.**

Prayer

Lord of truth, you speak with authority that frees hearts and minds. Open our ears to hear your word, strengthen us in courage to follow its call, and help us bring justice, mercy, and hope to the world, that your Spirit may transform our lives and our communities. **Amen.**

Gospel **Mark 1:21-28**

Then they came to Capernaum, and on the sabbath Jesus entered the synagogue and taught. The people were astonished at his teaching, for he taught them as one having authority and not as the scribes. In their synagogue was a man with an unclean spirit; he cried out, "What have you to do with us, Jesus of Nazareth? Have you come to destroy us? I know who you are—the Holy One of God!" Jesus rebuked him and said, "Quiet! Come out of him!" The unclean spirit convulsed him and with a loud cry came out of him. All were amazed and asked one another, "What is this? A new teaching with authority. He commands even the unclean spirits and they obey him." His fame spread everywhere throughout the whole region of Galilee.

Brief Silence

For Reflection

Last week's reflection urged readers that our welcome must be one that "meets people where they are and offers loving invitations . . ." This could be seen, potentially, as oppositional to a faith and a liturgical practice of it that speaks and lives truth (or *Truth*, with a capital T). The love that was spoken of last week and the truth that is spoken of in this week's gospel are of course not oppositional at all—God *is* love and God *is* truth, after all.

✦ Do you need Jesus to command anything of you? How can you be less afraid to ask him for help?

Brief Silence

Model Universal Prayer (Prayer of the Faithful)

We come before the Lord who always listens, quieting our hearts and bearing our hopes as we offer our prayers and petitions.

Response: Lord, hear our prayer.

For those living married lives of faith and love: may they take time and space to listen to and to love one another, we pray . . .

For families whose members are suffering from addictions: may they seek and find health and healing, we pray . . .

For those who have fallen away from their faith: may they hear Christ's teaching anew, and desire to try again, we pray . . .

For those suffering in persecution, darkness, and fear: may they be rescued from their captors and brought to safety, we pray . . .

O God, you sent your Son to call us out of darkness and the shadow of death. Do not allow our hearts to be hardened, but fill us with your compassion and mercy as we pray for all the world. We ask this through Christ our Lord. **Amen.**

Prayer

Spirit of wisdom, you speak truth that heals and restores. Help us hear your voice in our daily lives and follow where it leads. May our actions reflect your justice and compassion, drawing others to the light of your kingdom. **Amen.**

Gospel **Mark 1:29-39**

On leaving the synagogue Jesus entered the house of Simon and Andrew with James and John. Simon's mother-in-law lay sick with a fever. They immediately told him about her. He approached, grasped her hand, and helped her up. Then the fever left her and she waited on them.

When it was evening, after sunset, they brought to him all who were ill or possessed by demons. The whole town was gathered at the door. He cured many who were sick with various diseases, and he drove out many demons, not permitting them to speak because they knew him.

Rising very early before dawn, he left and went off to a deserted place, where he prayed. Simon and those who were with him pursued him and on finding him said, "Everyone is looking for you." He told them, "Let us go on to the nearby villages that I may preach there also. For this purpose have I come." So he went into their synagogues, preaching and driving out demons throughout the whole of Galilee.

Brief Silence

For Reflection

In today's gospel, Mark tells his readers about the power of Jesus's presence. It heals physically, it cures spiritually, and because of this, even when Jesus wishes more private time, he yields to the desire of those who yearn to be near him. Knowing what to do when in the presence of the Lord can be challenging, especially if it's our first time with a profound awareness of that presence. This includes those with whom we share our welcome to be disciples of Christ.

✦ Do you feel that Jesus is too busy to notice your pain? Knowing that he makes time for you, what healing do you want to ask of him?

Brief Silence

Model Universal Prayer (Prayer of the Faithful)

Coming before the Lord who hears us in our need, we offer our prayers and petitions.

Response: Lord, hear our prayer.

For the church: may the Holy Spirit fill the faithful with the fire of love and a thirst for justice and righteousness, we pray . . .

For nations whose leaders resort to intimidation and treachery to control their citizens: may God's justice call them to accountability, we pray . . .

For families who are suffering from economic instability: may they find solutions to sustain their loved ones, we pray . . .

For those gathered here today who are suffering in mind, body, or spirit: may the grace of God fill them with endurance and hope, we pray . . .

O God, you rebuild those who are broken and gather those who are scattered. Fill us with the hope of your healing and patience to know your wisdom. We ask this through Christ our Lord. **Amen.**

Prayer

God of restoration, you call us to return and be made whole. In this season of reflection, cleanse our hearts, heal our wounds, and renew our spirits, that we may walk humbly with you and bring your mercy and peace to a world in need of your love. **Amen.**

Gospel **Matt 6:1-6, 16-18**

Jesus said to his disciples: "Take care not to perform righteous deeds in order that people may see them; otherwise, you will have no recompense from your heavenly Father. When you give alms, do not blow a trumpet before you, as the hypocrites do in the synagogues and in the streets to win the praise of others. Amen, I say to you, they have received their reward. But when you give alms, do not let your left hand know what your right is doing, so that your almsgiving may be secret. And your Father who sees in secret will repay you.

"When you pray, do not be like the hypocrites, who love to stand and pray in the synagogues and on street corners so that others may see them. Amen, I say to you, they have received their reward. But when you pray, go to your inner room, close the door, and pray to your Father in secret. And your Father who sees in secret will repay you.

"When you fast, do not look gloomy like the hypocrites. They neglect their appearance, so that they may appear to others to be fasting. Amen, I say to you, they have received their reward. But when you fast, anoint your head and wash your face, so that you may not appear to be fasting, except to your Father who is hidden. And your Father who sees what is hidden will repay you."

Brief Silence

For Reflection

We have reached the season of Lent, so now is the time for all things sad and repentant and morose and sackcloth and ashes and everything else depressing, right? No! We ought to be repentant for our sinfulness, yes. But there's more to the story. It's not like during Lent we should remember only repentance, suffering, and death. While celebrating these things, we should also remember that there is new life that arises from these very same things—there is joy and even more celebrating to come.

✦ How have you experienced joy in repentance, conversion, and "doing better"?

Brief Silence

Model Universal Prayer (Prayer of the Faithful)

Let us bring our prayers and petitions before the Lord who hears us in our need.

Response: Lord, hear our prayer.

For the church: may we begin this Lenten season with fortitude and hope, desiring a renewal of our hearts, we pray . . .

For our leaders at home and in our nation: may they govern with justice and protect their people with mercy, we pray . . .

For those whose hearts are burdened by sadness: may they find the presence of the Lord walking with them as we journey toward Easter, we pray . . .

For all those gathered here today: may the ashes we have received remind us that we are made and loved by God, we pray . . .

Lord God, you call your people to enter into this holy season of Lent. May we remember we are dust, and remember our call to extend mercy to all that we meet. We ask this through Christ our Lord. **Amen.**

Prayer

Jesus, source of strength, you faced the desert with steadfast love and trust in your Father. Help us turn from what leads us astray. May we find our sustenance in your word, and walk faithfully in your ways, bringing light and hope to the lives we touch. **Amen.**

Gospel **Mark 1:12-15**

The Spirit drove Jesus out into the desert, and he remained in the desert for forty days, tempted by Satan. He was among wild beasts, and the angels ministered to him.

After John had been arrested, Jesus came to Galilee proclaiming the gospel of God: "This is the time of fulfillment. The kingdom of God is at hand. Repent, and believe in the gospel."

Brief Silence

For Reflection

It's easy to imagine Satan waiting for just the right moment, when he knew Jesus would be at his weakest. Satan presents Jesus with versions of sacred power and might that have been twisted and distorted. Persevering through the trial, Jesus begins his earthly mission by proclaiming the immediacy of the reign of God, that the old covenants of God are coming to fulfillment. Jesus's words and deeds over the next three years will make it clear that he is the living embodiment of God, the new and everlasting covenant.

✦ How can your Lent be a time of fulfillment? How can you embrace this time of "desert fasting" with joy?

Brief Silence

Model Universal Prayer (Prayer of the Faithful)

We bring our prayers before the Lord, who remembers his faithfulness always.

Response: Lord, hear our prayer.

For the church, especially where our brothers and sisters in Christ are suffering from persecution and oppression, we pray . . .

For nations whose people are afraid for their safety and the safety of their loved ones, we pray . . .

For communities suffering from the effects of climate change with drought, flooding, heat, and cold, we pray . . .

For all who have been entrapped by habits of sin and destruction, we pray . . .

O God, in your goodness you remember your people. Hear our prayers and petitions this day for ourselves and all the world, and may we work to spread love for your justice. We ask this through Christ our Lord. **Amen.**

Prayer

God of radiant light, in Christ you unveil the beauty and goodness hidden within us. Illuminate our hearts and guide our steps in your ways. Let the brilliance of your love transform our lives, so that we may shine with your presence. **Amen.**

Gospel **Mark 9:2-10**

Jesus took Peter, James, and John and led them up a high mountain apart by themselves. And he was transfigured before them, and his clothes became dazzling white, such as no fuller on earth could bleach them. Then Elijah appeared to them along with Moses, and they were conversing with Jesus. Then Peter said to Jesus in reply, "Rabbi, it is good that we are here! Let us make three tents: one for you, one for Moses, and one for Elijah." He hardly knew what to say, they were so terrified. Then a cloud came, casting a shadow over them; from the cloud came a voice, "This is my beloved Son. Listen to him." Suddenly, looking around, they no longer saw anyone but Jesus alone with them.

As they were coming down from the mountain, he charged them not to relate what they had seen to anyone, except when the Son of Man had risen from the dead. So they kept the matter to themselves, questioning what rising from the dead meant.

Brief Silence

For Reflection

On this Sunday of Lent in each lectionary cycle, we always hear about the transfiguration of the Lord, one of the few passages found in each of the three Synoptic Gospels, and a moment even alluded to in Peter's second epistle. Jesus's clothes become dazzlingly white, Mark tells us, and Luke's Gospel adds that Jesus's face shone brightly like the sun. Light, considered together with darkness, is an always present sign and symbol of our faith. There is no darkness the light cannot overcome, John's beautiful prologue reminds us.

✦ What does Jesus's transfiguration say to you? How might this miracle teach you something about Jesus?

Brief Silence

Model Universal Prayer (Prayer of the Faithful)

Lord God, your light is revealed in the face of Christ, who suffered and died for us. Confident that you are with us and hear us always, we offer you our petitions this day.

Response: Lord, hear our prayer.

For the bishops and pastors of the church: may they always seek to teach the fullness of the law and prophets in Christ crucified, we pray . . .

For the civil leaders of our country and our world: may the law of God inform their judgments and actions, we pray . . .

For those who are persecuted under unjust uses of the law: may they find God's freedom and justice, we pray . . .

For all those here: may we embrace the prophetic task of proclaiming truth and mercy in our daily lives, we pray . . .

Lord, you hear us as a father hears his children. We trust in your justice and mercy as we bring these prayers to you. We ask this through Christ our Lord. **Amen.**

Prayer

God of living water, you meet us in our longing and quench our thirst for meaning and peace. Open our hearts to your grace and refresh our spirits with your presence. Teach us to receive and share the gift of life that flows from you. **Amen.**

Gospel **John 2:13-25**

Since the Passover of the Jews was near, Jesus went up to Jerusalem. He found in the temple area those who sold oxen, sheep, and doves, as well as the money changers seated there. He made a whip out of cords and drove them all out of the temple area, with the sheep and oxen, and spilled the coins of the money changers and overturned their tables, and to those who sold doves he said, "Take these out of here, and stop making my Father's house a marketplace." His disciples recalled the words of Scripture, *Zeal for your house will consume me.* At this the Jews answered and said to him, "What sign can you show us for doing this?" Jesus answered and said to them, "Destroy this temple and in three days I will raise it up." The Jews said, "This temple has been under construction for forty-six years, and you will raise it up in three days?" But he was speaking about the temple of his body. Therefore, when he was raised from the dead, his disciples remembered that he had said this, and they came to believe the Scripture and the word Jesus had spoken.

While he was in Jerusalem for the feast of Passover, many began to believe in his name when they saw the signs he was doing. But Jesus would not trust himself to them because he knew them all, and did not need anyone to testify about human nature. He himself understood it well.

Brief Silence

For Reflection

In today's gospel, we see Jesus filled with righteous anger as he drives out the money changers from the temple. This image—zealous and forceful—can feel jarring when we're used to seeing Jesus as the Good Shepherd or the Prince of Peace. But it's an important reminder: God is more than any one image or role. If we only ever see God as distant Creator or Almighty Judge, we risk missing the fullness of God's identity. This fullness is made known in Jesus Christ, fully God and fully human.

✦ Have you ever experienced righteous anger in yourself or others? What was the occasion?

Brief Silence

Model Universal Prayer (Prayer of the Faithful)

The precepts of the Lord are right, rejoicing the heart. Let us trust in the Lord, whose laws are perfect and whose kindness is everlasting

Response: Lord, hear our prayer.

That zeal for our faith might consume the church, drawing us into communion with one another, rather than self-righteousness and division, we pray . . .

That our lawmakers and government officials may seek guidance in the wisdom and justice of God, we pray . . .

That all who feel cast off and divided from their homes, their families, or their communities might find new hope and restoration in their lives, we pray . . .

That we might reject vengeance and violence fed by hatred, and instead fill our hearts with the merciful love of God, we pray . . .

O God, you alone have the words of everlasting life. May we be filled with zeal for your love and for the care and protection of our neighbors. We ask this through Christ our Lord. **Amen.**

Prayer

Christ, radiance of mercy, you shine into the shadows of our hearts. Help us turn fully to you and embrace your healing touch. May we live in the freedom and joy that come from walking in your light. **Amen.**

Gospel **John 3:14-21**

Jesus said to Nicodemus: "Just as Moses lifted up the serpent in the desert, so must the Son of Man be lifted up, so that everyone who believes in him may have eternal life."

For God so loved the world that he gave his only Son, so that everyone who believes in him might not perish but might have eternal life. For God did not send his Son into the world to condemn the world, but that the world might be saved through him. Whoever believes in him will not be condemned, but whoever does not believe has already been condemned, because he has not believed in the name of the only Son of God. And this is the verdict, that the light came into the world, but people preferred darkness to light, because their works were evil. For everyone who does wicked things hates the light and does not come toward the light, so that his works might not be exposed. But whoever lives the truth comes to the light, so that his works may be clearly seen as one in God.

Brief Silence

For Reflection

John 3:16 is a familiar passage from today's gospel: "For God so loved the world that he gave his only Son, so that everyone who believes in him might not perish but might have eternal life." This eternal life is offered to us as a gift. It is nothing to be earned or bought; it can only be gratefully received. The immensity of God's love for us is represented both in what the gift is—eternal life with God—and by the gift of God sending his Son to us.

✦ Do you believe that Jesus brings eternal life? Does anything worry you about your own salvation?

Brief Silence

Model Universal Prayer (Prayer of the Faithful)

God, you are the source of our life and salvation. Confident that you hear us and want us in your light, we offer to you our needs and petitions.

Response: Lord, hear our prayer.

For the leaders of our world, especially leaders of international bodies for relief and peacekeeping, that they might be inspired to bring God's light to those places marked by violence and war, we pray . . .

For this nation's leaders, that they might lead, speak, and guide according to the truth, we pray . . .

For those who struggle with the truth of their addictions, harmful actions, and hurtful relationships, we pray . . .

For the members of our community, that they might always find themselves in the healing light of God, we pray . . .

Living God, you are light unending and truth eternal. We ask you to hear our prayers and to help us to walk in your ways. We ask this though Christ our Lord. **Amen.**

Prayer

God of life, you call us from the shadows into your presence. Strengthen our trust in your power and awaken hope in our hearts. Let us believe in your promise of new life and live each day in the light of your love. **Amen.**

Gospel **John 12:20-33**

Some Greeks who had come to worship at the Passover Feast came to Philip, who was from Bethsaida in Galilee, and asked him, "Sir, we would like to see Jesus." Philip went and told Andrew; then Andrew and Philip went and told Jesus. Jesus answered them, "The hour has come for the Son of Man to be glorified. Amen, amen, I say to you, unless a grain of wheat falls to the ground and dies, it remains just a grain of wheat; but if it dies, it produces much fruit. Whoever loves his life loses it, and whoever hates his life in this world will preserve it for eternal life. Whoever serves me must follow me, and where I am, there also will my servant be. The Father will honor whoever serves me.

"I am troubled now. Yet what should I say? 'Father, save me from this hour'? But it was for this purpose that I came to this hour. Father, glorify your name." Then a voice came from heaven, "I have glorified it and will glorify it again." The crowd there heard it and said it was thunder; but others said, "An angel has spoken to him." Jesus answered and said, "This voice did not come for my sake but for yours. Now is the time of judgment on this world; now the ruler of this world will be driven out. And when I am lifted up from the earth, I will draw everyone to myself." He said this indicating the kind of death he would die.

Brief Silence

For Reflection

On this Sunday we hear that there are days coming when God will make a new covenant, where God's laws will not be handed on to us externally, like the Ten Commandments on tablets, but will be written on our hearts. In the gospel, we are told of God's thunderous voice, much like the voice at the transfiguration. Everything seems to return us to where the journey began: Jesus's proclamation that the kingdom of God is at hand.

✦ What does Jesus's courage teach you today? How can you model it in your own life this week?

Brief Silence

Model Universal Prayer (Prayer of the Faithful)

Seeking always to glorify God's name, we offer our prayers and petitions for ourselves and for all the world.

Response: Lord, hear our prayer.

For the church this Lenten season: may it be filled with the Holy Spirit, new life, and hope for the future, we pray . . .

For all who have devoted their lives to serving their communities: may they find abundant blessing in their work and peace in their hearts, we pray . . .

For those who feel directionless and long to know the Lord: may they encounter him in the word, in the sacraments, and in the witness of all the faithful, we pray . . .

For those among us and in our community preparing for baptism, confirmation, and full communion with the Catholic Church: may their prayers and supplications be heard as they approach the sacraments of initiation, we pray . . .

Merciful God, you draw all people to yourself. Hear our prayers as we offer them to you and help us to grow in perfect obedience to your will. We ask this through Christ our Lord. **Amen.**

PALM SUNDAY OF THE PASSION OF THE LORD

Prayer

Christ our King, Hosanna in the highest! You enter our lives with gentle glory. Grant us hearts ready to honor you, hands willing to serve, and the grace to walk faithfully with you, sharing your love and hope in all we do. **Amen.**

Gospel **Mark 15:1–39 (or Mark 14:1–15:47)**

As soon as morning came, the chief priests with the elders and the scribes, that is, the whole Sanhedrin held a council. They bound Jesus, led him away, and handed him over to Pilate. Pilate questioned him, "Are you the king of the Jews?" He said to him in reply, "You say so." The chief priests accused him of many things. Again Pilate questioned him, "Have you no answer? See how many things they accuse you of." Jesus gave him no further answer, so that Pilate was amazed.

Now on the occasion of the feast he used to release to them one prisoner whom they requested. A man called Barabbas was then in prison along with the rebels who had committed murder in a rebellion. The crowd came forward and began to ask him to do for them as he was accustomed. Pilate answered, "Do you want me to release to you the king of the Jews?" For he knew that it was out of envy that the chief priests had handed him over. But the chief priests stirred up the crowd to have him release Barabbas for them instead. Pilate again said to them in reply, "Then what do you want me to do with the man you call the king of the Jews?" They shouted again, "Crucify him." Pilate said to them, "Why? What evil has he done?" They only shouted the louder, "Crucify him." So Pilate, wishing to satisfy the crowd, released

Barabbas to them and, after he had Jesus scourged, handed him over to be crucified.

The soldiers led him away inside the palace, that is, the praetorium, and assembled the whole cohort. They clothed him in purple and, weaving a crown of thorns, placed it on him. They began to salute him with, "Hail, King of the Jews!" and kept striking his head with a reed and spitting upon him. They knelt before him in homage. And when they had mocked him, they stripped him of the purple cloak, dressed him in his own clothes, and led him out to crucify him.

They pressed into service a passer-by, Simon, a Cyrenian, who was coming in from the country, the father of Alexander and Rufus, to carry his cross.

They brought him to the place of Golgotha—which is translated Place of the Skull—. They gave him wine drugged with myrrh, but he did not take it. Then they crucified him and divided his garments by casting lots for them to see what each should take. It was nine o'clock in the morning when they crucified him. The inscription of the charge against him read, "The King of the Jews." With him they crucified two revolutionaries, one on his right and one on his left. Those passing by reviled him, shaking their heads and saying, "Aha! You who would destroy the temple and rebuild it in three days, save yourself by coming down from the cross." Likewise the chief priests, with the scribes, mocked him among themselves and said, "He saved others; he cannot save himself. Let the Christ, the King of Israel, come down now from the cross that we may see and believe." Those who were crucified with him also kept abusing him.

At noon darkness came over the whole land until three in the afternoon. And at three o'clock Jesus cried out in a loud voice, *"Eloi, Eloi, lema sabachthani?"* which is translated, "My God, my God, why have you forsaken me?" Some of the bystanders who heard it said, "Look, he is calling Elijah." One of them ran, soaked a sponge with wine, put it on a reed and gave it to him to drink saying, "Wait, let us see if Elijah comes to take him down." Jesus gave a loud cry and breathed his last.

Here all kneel and pause for a short time.

The veil of the sanctuary was torn in two from top to bottom. When the centurion who stood facing him saw how he breathed his last he said, "Truly this man was the Son of God!"

Brief Silence

For Reflection

It might be easily overlooked how often Jesus goes from place to place: the entrance into Jerusalem, to the Passover supper, the agony in the garden, the trial, to Pilate, to the stripping and mocking, to his crucifixion. Each of these is a procession. Jesus's many processions are linked to our own. Our earthly travels mirror his: visiting friends, dining, sharing good news, and more. Our spiritual travels mirror his: pilgrimages through both the joys and sorrows of life, with the goal of eternal unity with God and God's people.

✦ Is there something in your life for which you need anointing, healing, or prayers? Whom can you invite into your life who might be able to help?

Brief Silence

Model Universal Prayer (Prayer of the Faithful)

We offer our prayers and petitions to God who hears us in our need (petitions drawn from *Fratelli Tutti* 5, 9-19).
Response: Lord, hear our prayer.

That the church might serve as a light to the nations, calling all to care for our elderly and our young, and honoring the dignity of all human persons, we pray . . .

That nations who are consumed by selfishness and aggressive ideologies might give way to goodness, love, justice, and solidarity, we pray . . .

That those who choose violence and destruction of life might be freed from the snares of evil which entrap them, we pray . . .

That our community and all gathered here may join in caring for creation, remembering that our whole human family dwells in a common home, we pray . . .

God, creator of all, you have called human beings to live as brothers and sisters. In the sight of the unbounded mercy of your Son's passion, may we bind ourselves in solidarity with all the world. We ask this through Christ our Lord. **Amen.**

HOLY THURSDAY EVENING MASS OF THE LORD'S SUPPER

Prayer

Jesus, servant of all, you gave us your body and blood as a sign of love. Teach us to serve one another with humble hearts and to break bread in gratitude. Help us to follow your example of selfless care, that we may live your command to love without measure. **Amen.**

Gospel **John 13:1-15**

Before the feast of Passover, Jesus knew that his hour had come to pass from this world to the Father. He loved his own in the world and he loved them to the end. The devil had already induced Judas, son of Simon the Iscariot, to hand him over. So, during supper, fully aware that the Father had put everything into his power and that he had come from God and was returning to God, he rose from supper and took off his outer garments. He took a towel and tied it around his waist. Then he poured water into a basin and began to wash the disciples' feet and dry them with the towel around his waist. He came to Simon Peter, who said to him, "Master, are you going to wash my feet?" Jesus answered and said to him, "What I am doing, you do not understand now, but you will understand later." Peter said to him, "You will never wash my feet." Jesus answered him, "Unless I wash you, you will have no inheritance with me." Simon Peter said to him, "Master, then not only my feet, but my hands and head as well." Jesus said to him, "Whoever has bathed has no need except to have his feet washed, for he is clean all over; so you are clean, but not all." For he knew who would betray him; for this reason, he said, "Not all of you are clean."

So when he had washed their feet and put his garments back on and reclined at table again, he said to them, "Do you realize what I have done for you? You call me 'teacher' and 'master,' and rightly so, for indeed I am. If I, therefore, the master and teacher, have washed your feet, you ought to wash one another's feet. I have given you a model to follow, so that as I have done for you, you should also do."

Brief Silence

For Reflection

The liturgy itself links the eucharistic meal to that which those who partake in it must be and must do. The followers of Christ must be humble servants, giving of themselves as the least among their peers. This is what it means to be in Christian community: each member in Christ's body should be a humble, generous servant to one another. This is where unity is found—not in any uniformity of language or appearance, but in love, perfectly demonstrated by God's own Son.

✦ How do you experience unity in the act of eucharistic Communion: at Mass, in bringing Communion to the sick and homebound, or in receiving Communion while homebound or in a health facility?

Brief Silence

(continued)

HOLY THURSDAY EVENING MASS OF THE LORD'S SUPPER

Model Universal Prayer (Prayer of the Faithful)

Turning to the Lord as we enter his paschal mystery, we pray . . .

Response: Lord, hear our prayer.

For our bishops, priests, and deacons: may the Lord who has called them to serve the faithful in word and sacrament be always present in their lives, we pray . . .

For peace among nations: may we who have learned from the model of Christ Jesus be agents of his love in the world, we pray . . .

For those who have turned away from their faith: may they feel the prompting of the Spirit during this holy time, we pray . . .

For all gathered here, especially those awaiting the sacraments of initiation: may they feel the love of the Lord, we pray . . .

O God, you gave your only Son so that we might have eternal life. Hear our prayers this holy night, and lead us ever closer to your Son, Jesus Christ our Lord, who lives and reigns with you and the Holy Spirit, God forever and ever. **Amen.**

EASTER SUNDAY OF THE RESURRECTION AT THE MASS DURING THE DAY

Prayer

Risen Lord, source of new life, you have conquered death. Awaken our hearts to your triumph, strengthen us to share your joy, and let the power of your rising from the dead transform our lives so we may reflect your glory and love in all we do. **Amen.**

Gospel **John 20:1-9 (or Mark 16:1-7; or at an afternoon or evening Mass, Luke 24:13-35)**

On the first day of the week, Mary of Magdala came to the tomb early in the morning, while it was still dark, and saw the stone removed from the tomb. So she ran and went to Simon Peter and to the other disciple whom Jesus loved, and told them, "They have taken the Lord from the tomb, and we don't know where they put him." So Peter and the other disciple went out and came to the tomb. They both ran, but the other disciple ran faster than Peter and arrived at the tomb first; he bent down and saw the burial cloths there, but did not go in. When Simon Peter arrived after him, he went into the tomb and saw the burial cloths there, and the cloth that had covered his head, not with the burial cloths but rolled up in a separate place. Then the other disciple also went in, the one who had arrived at the tomb first, and he saw and believed. For they did not yet understand the Scripture that he had to rise from the dead.

Brief Silence

For Reflection

In John's telling of the discovery of the resurrection he points out that "the other disciple whom Jesus loved" ran faster than Peter to the tomb. While John arrives at the tomb first, he does not enter. Rather, it is the typically impetuous Peter who enters to examine the scene. All of this happens, though, because Mary of Magdala runs to them first, having been the first to see the stone rolled away. As Apostle to the Apostles, the first kerygma belongs to her.

✦ What is the most convincing way for you to hear the kerygma, the message of Christ's death and resurrection: A hymn? A homily? A work of art?

Brief Silence

Model Universal Prayer (Prayer of the Faithful)

Turning with confidence to the Lord we offer our prayers and petitions.

Response: Lord, hear our prayer.

For the church: may the joy of Easter widen our hearts and deepen our love for one another, we pray . . .

For our public servants, health care workers, and first responders: may those charged with caring for their communities receive abundant blessings, we pray . . .

For all who are alone this day: may we who are blessed with community recognize them, we pray . . .

For all who have received sacraments of initiation this Easter: may Easter joy continue to enliven and enrich their lives, we pray . . .

O God, you are giver of life and source of all things good. Hear our prayers this joyous day, and fill our hearts with trust that you will answer all our needs. We ask this through Christ our Lord. **Amen.**

SECOND SUNDAY OF EASTER (OR OF DIVINE MERCY)

Prayer

Jesus, fountain of mercy, you breathe peace into hearts weighed down by fear and doubt. Open our eyes to your tenderness and awaken our trust in your forgiving love. Lead us to share your gentle compassion with others, that your mercy may ripple through every life we touch. **Amen.**

Gospel **John 20:19-31**

On the evening of that first day of the week, when the doors were locked, where the disciples were, for fear of the Jews, Jesus came and stood in their midst and said to them, "Peace be with you." When he had said this, he showed them his hands and his side. The disciples rejoiced when they saw the Lord. Jesus said to them again, "Peace be with you. As the Father has sent me, so I send you." And when he had said this, he breathed on them and said to them, "Receive the Holy Spirit. Whose sins you forgive are forgiven them, and whose sins you retain are retained."

Thomas, called Didymus, one of the Twelve, was not with them when Jesus came. So the other disciples said to him, "We have seen the Lord." But he said to them, "Unless I see the mark of the nails in his hands and put my finger into the nailmarks and put my hand into his side, I will not believe."

Now a week later his disciples were again inside and Thomas was with them. Jesus came, although the doors were locked, and stood in their midst and said, "Peace be with you." Then he said to Thomas, "Put your finger here and see my hands, and bring your hand and put it into my side, and do not be unbelieving, but believe." Thomas answered and said to him, "My Lord and my God!" Jesus said to him, "Have you come to believe because you have seen me? Blessed are those who have not seen and have believed."

Now, Jesus did many other signs in the presence of his disciples that are not written in this book. But these are written that you may come to believe that Jesus is the Christ, the Son of God, and that through this belief you may have life in his name.

Brief Silence

For Reflection

It is on this Second Sunday of Easter each year when we hear about the apostle Thomas and his first encounter with the risen Lord. Christ's resurrected and glorified body certainly could have been made completely whole again, yet the wounds of the nails and spear persist, and Thomas is able to touch and feel them. "My Lord and my God!" he cries. Here Christ is truly a wounded healer—and beyond that, a teacher, a friend, and a brother.

✦ Like Thomas, did you ever feel left out or find yourself doubtful about an experience you didn't share?

Brief Silence

Model Universal Prayer (Prayer of the Faithful)

Believing in the wondrous power of God, we bring our prayers and petitions before him.

Response: Lord, hear our prayer.

For the church: may we become a community of believers of one heart and mind, growing in patience and holiness, we pray . . .

For leaders of nations: may their governing promote the care for the common good and protection of the innocent, we pray . . .

For those who are suffering: may they find comfort in the mystery of Christ and care in the love of their neighbors, we pray . . .

For all gathered here today: may we testify to the love of the Lord through our mercy toward those around us, we pray . . .

O God, when we love you and obey your commandments, we make you known throughout the world. May we follow you always, filled by your Spirit and testifying to your truth. We ask this through Christ our Lord. **Amen.**

Prayer

Jesus, companion of the journey, you walk with us in every path we take. Help us to recognize your voice, trust your guidance, and live each day with hearts alert to your nearness, finding joy in the simplicity of your faithful and sustaining presence. **Amen.**

Gospel **Luke 24:35-48**

The two disciples recounted what had taken place on the way, and how Jesus was made known to them in the breaking of bread.

While they were still speaking about this, he stood in their midst and said to them, "Peace be with you." But they were startled and terrified and thought that they were seeing a ghost. Then he said to them, "Why are you troubled? And why do questions arise in your hearts? Look at my hands and my feet, that it is I myself. Touch me and see, because a ghost does not have flesh and bones as you can see I have." And as he said this, he showed them his hands and his feet. While they were still incredulous for joy and were amazed, he asked them, "Have you anything here to eat? " They gave him a piece of baked fish; he took it and ate it in front of them.

He said to them, "These are my words that I spoke to you while I was still with you, that everything written about me in the law of Moses and in the prophets and psalms must be fulfilled." Then he opened their minds to understand the Scriptures. And he said to them, "Thus it is written that the Christ would suffer and rise from the dead on the third day and that repentance, for the forgiveness of sins, would be preached in his name to all the nations, beginning from Jerusalem. You are witnesses of these things."

Brief Silence

For Reflection

Up until now, the good news of Christ's resurrection was primarily shared among friends and relatives, a very close circle of those who surrounded Jesus himself during his three years of ministry. We are at a "hinge" moment of the narrative, and of our Easter season, when Christ, in the last line of the gospel, reminds the apostles that it is their ministry, foretold by the prophets, to share the joy of the resurrection and forgiveness of sins with all nations. We too must consider how we do that ourselves.

✦ Has Jesus ever surprised you by meeting you along your way?

Brief Silence

Model Universal Prayer (Prayer of the Faithful)

We trust that the Lord does wonders for his faithful, and hears all who call upon him. Let us come before him with joy and hope as we bring our prayers and petitions.

Response: Lord, hear our prayer.

For the church this Easter season, and for our Orthodox brothers and sisters throughout the world: may we rejoice together in the glory of the Risen Lord, we pray . . .

For nations throughout the world, especially those whose citizens lack security, confidence, and peace: may their leaders reject corruption and seek righteousness, we pray . . .

For refugees and migrants who are afraid for their safety and the safety of their loved ones: may they feel Christ's presence in the support of those who help them, we pray . . .

For all gathered here, especially those who have received the sacraments of initiation during this Easter season: may they find continued strength in their new life in Christ, we pray . . .

O God, you made your justice known through the paschal mystery of your Son, Jesus Christ. May we rejoice in your love this Easter season, and make your salvation known as we work for justice throughout the world. We ask this through Christ our Lord. **Amen.**

Prayer

Shepherd of all, you guide us to green pastures and calm waters. Teach us to hear your voice above the noise and to follow where you lead. Help us to rest in the safety of your care, finding courage and peace in your unfailing love and tender protection. **Amen.**

Gospel **John 10:11-18**

Jesus said: "I am the good shepherd. A good shepherd lays down his life for the sheep. A hired man, who is not a shepherd and whose sheep are not his own, sees a wolf coming and leaves the sheep and runs away, and the wolf catches and scatters them. This is because he works for pay and has no concern for the sheep. I am the good shepherd, and I know mine and mine know me, just as the Father knows me and I know the Father; and I will lay down my life for the sheep. I have other sheep that do not belong to this fold. These also I must lead, and they will hear my voice, and there will be one flock, one shepherd. This is why the Father loves me, because I lay down my life in order to take it up again. No one takes it from me, but I lay it down on my own. I have power to lay it down, and power to take it up again. This command I have received from my Father."

Brief Silence

For Reflection

Though the imagery is not as prevalent in this cycle of readings, it is still Good Shepherd Sunday, the gospel reminds us. While we might wish to imagine the good shepherd as the one who, upon finding the lost sheep, lovingly hoists it over his shoulders to bring it back to the other ninety-nine, this is not the shepherd Jesus speaks of today. This good shepherd has to protect the flock from wolves—and lays down his life to do so.

✦ Can you make space for Christ, so that he can protect you? Do others in your life need you, likewise, to protect them?

Brief Silence

Model Universal Prayer (Prayer of the Faithful)

The Lord, the rock of our salvation, hears our cries and showers us with his eternal graces. Let us offer our needs and petitions to him this day.

Response: Lord, hear our prayer.

For Pope N. and all the bishops of the church: may they lead with the humility and steadfastness of shepherds, we pray . . .

For the leaders of nations: may they steward their people with loving care, we pray . . .

For local civic officials: may they embrace their office as an opportunity for service, we pray . . .

For those gathered here: may the light of the resurrection inspire us to faithful service of our neighbors, we pray . . .

Loving God, you care for your flock with tenderness and joy. Hear our prayers, which we humbly offer to you. We ask this through Christ our Lord. **Amen.**

Prayer

God of tender growth, you weave us into your vineyard of life. Help us remain close to you, bearing the fruits of faithful love. Lead us to support one another with generosity and hope, discovering the richness of your life flowing through us and shaping our hearts in your image. **Amen.**

Gospel **John 15:1-8**

Jesus said to his disciples: "I am the true vine, and my Father is the vine grower. He takes away every branch in me that does not bear fruit, and every one that does he prunes so that it bears more fruit. You are already pruned because of the word that I spoke to you. Remain in me, as I remain in you. Just as a branch cannot bear fruit on its own unless it remains on the vine, so neither can you unless you remain in me. I am the vine, you are the branches. Whoever remains in me and I in him will bear much fruit, because without me you can do nothing. Anyone who does not remain in me will be thrown out like a branch and wither; people will gather them and throw them into a fire and they will be burned. If you remain in me and my words remain in you, ask for whatever you want and it will be done for you. By this is my Father glorified, that you bear much fruit and become my disciples."

Brief Silence

For Reflection

In today's gospel, Jesus reminds us that sometimes his Father prunes the vine so that it may bear more fruit. If you are feeling particularly stretched this year, it may be time for some pruning. Consider starting a list of the various responsibilities and tasks you have to do each day. In a month or two, look at that list and see where opportunities may exist to prune the vine. Be prepared for some initial pain amid the pruning, trusting the Lord that more abundant fruit lies ahead.

✦ Are you, or someone you know, feeling cut off from Christ? Why so?

Brief Silence

Model Universal Prayer (Prayer of the Faithful)

Let us have confidence in the Lord as we come before him with our prayers and petitions.

Response: Lord, hear our prayer.

For the church this Easter season: may we be filled with new peace and the unity to which your Son calls us, we pray . . .

For all nations, especially those suffering from conflict and violence: may they find justice and protection in you, we pray . . .

For all who have been baptized, confirmed, and have received their first Eucharist this Easter season: may they be filled with the grace of Christ and find confidence in their new life of faith, we pray . . .

For our community assembled here today: may we find assurance that God is greater than our hearts can imagine, we pray . . .

God our Father, your Son gave us your command to love one another as he has loved us. May we keep your command to love, and allow the Spirit he gave us to dwell more deeply within us. We ask this through Christ our Lord. **Amen.**

Prayer

Spirit of truth, you dwell within us and guide our hearts in every decision. Open our minds to your wisdom, strengthen us to live in love, and help us keep the path of Christ, discovering joy and freedom in following his commandments with trust and hope. **Amen.**

Gospel **John 15:9-17**

Jesus said to his disciples: "As the Father loves me, so I also love you. Remain in my love. If you keep my commandments, you will remain in my love, just as I have kept my Father's commandments and remain in his love.

"I have told you this so that my joy may be in you and your joy might be complete. This is my commandment: love one another as I love you. No one has greater love than this, to lay down one's life for one's friends. You are my friends if you do what I command you. I no longer call you slaves, because a slave does not know what his master is doing. I have called you friends, because I have told you everything I have heard from my Father. It was not you who chose me, but I who chose you and appointed you to go and bear fruit that will remain, so that whatever you ask the Father in my name he may give you. This I command you: love one another."

Brief Silence

For Reflection

To be called a friend of Jesus is to be drawn into the very heart of divine love. Yet it also carries responsibility. Jesus immediately connects this new friendship with the commandment to love one another as he has loved us. Friendship with Christ is not a private privilege; it is the soil from which self-giving love must grow. We are chosen and appointed to bear fruit—fruit that will last—by living out that same sacrificial love that defined Jesus's life and death.

✦ Are you withholding anything from Christ? Is your church or home community withholding anything from Christ?

Brief Silence

Model Universal Prayer (Prayer of the Faithful)

The God of love calls us to follow in his ways. As we journey towards God, we offer the hopes and needs of our community this day.

Response: Lord, hear our prayer.

For the universal church: may it be a sign of God's love from age to age, we pray . . .

For all engaged in global trade: may they treat their partners with justice and dignity, we pray . . .

For those who reside in our own country, especially those who suffer from lack of resources: may they be graced with access to local food sources and a just market, we pray . . .

For all gathered here: may the love of Christ unite us in the work of the Gospel, we pray . . .

Father of compassion, see our strivings and hear our prayers with mercy. Grant that, from end to end, our world might be touched by your covenantal love. We ask this through Christ our Lord. **Amen.**

THE ASCENSION OF THE LORD

Prayer

Lord of heaven and earth, you lift your gaze from the clouds and invite us to look beyond ourselves. Strengthen our hearts to trust in your promises, inspire us to share your love boldly, and fill our lives with the hope of your abiding promise.
Amen.

Gospel **Mark 16:15-20**

Jesus said to his disciples: "Go into the whole world and proclaim the gospel to every creature. Whoever believes and is baptized will be saved; whoever does not believe will be condemned. These signs will accompany those who believe: in my name they will drive out demons, they will speak new languages. They will pick up serpents with their hands, and if they drink any deadly thing, it will not harm them. They will lay hands on the sick, and they will recover."

So then the Lord Jesus, after he spoke to them, was taken up into heaven and took his seat at the right hand of God. But they went forth and preached everywhere, while the Lord worked with them and confirmed the word through accompanying signs.

Brief Silence

For Reflection

Jesus's death and resurrection earned for us a new life, but we're not there yet. His ascension shows us that where he has gone, we one day hope to follow—but not yet. "Already, not yet" is one of the often-overlooked paradoxes of our Christian faith. This odd in-between time can be hard to wrap our heads around. But isn't that the ultimate goal, as recited in the Creed every Sunday: the resurrection of the dead *and* the life of the world to come?

✦ What does the "life of the world to come" mean to you? How can it make a difference to how we live day-to-day in this life?

Brief Silence

Model Universal Prayer (Prayer of the Faithful)

Trusting in the Lord who calls us to believe in his goodness, we pray . . .

Response: Lord, hear our prayer.

For the church throughout the world: may we grow in greater unity, equipping our ministers, lay and ordained, for the work of building up the Body of Christ, we pray . . .

For all nations, especially for those struggling with religious tensions and persecution: may faith in the living God inspire peace and compromise so that all faiths might live in harmony, we pray . . .

For those serving as missionaries and ministers in dangerous situations: may they be protected in their work of bringing the gospel of peace to the faithful, we pray . . .

For all gathered here: may we reject temptations to divide our hearts from our neighbors who are different than ourselves, we pray . . .

O God, you are king above all the earth and reign over the nations. Rule over our hearts so that we might always sing your praises, be agents of peace, and draw all peoples to you. We ask this through Christ our Lord. **Amen.**

Prayer

Father of glory, you have lifted your Son and filled the heavens with light. Draw our hearts into the unity he prayed for. Strengthen us to witness his love, and guide us in living as one people, faithful in hope and steadfast in trust. **Amen.**

Gospel **John 17:11b-19**

Lifting up his eyes to heaven, Jesus prayed, saying: "Holy Father, keep them in your name that you have given me, so that they may be one just as we are one. When I was with them I protected them in your name that you gave me, and I guarded them, and none of them was lost except the son of destruction, in order that the Scripture might be fulfilled. But now I am coming to you. I speak this in the world so that they may share my joy completely. I gave them your word, and the world hated them, because they do not belong to the world any more than I belong to the world. I do not ask that you take them out of the world but that you keep them from the evil one. They do not belong to the world any more than I belong to the world. Consecrate them in the truth. Your word is truth. As you sent me into the world, so I sent them into the world. And I consecrate myself for them, so that they also may be consecrated in truth."

Brief Silence

For Reflection

The gospel today is indeed Jesus praying, as if a presider over his community. He asks his Father that "they may share my joy completely" and that he "keep them from the evil one." Not invoked by name in this pericope, Jesus had just spoken of the coming Advocate, and we may safely link the Holy Spirit to these prayers for joy, security, and unity. If we are to pray what we believe and believe what we pray, let us all give these orations the attention and intelligibility they need.

✦ Do you believe that you can bring unity into the lives of others? How can you grow in this belief, with Christ and in the Holy Spirit?

Brief Silence

Model Universal Prayer (Prayer of the Faithful)

Jesus came into the world so that the world might be saved. Trusting in his promise, we turn to him with our prayers and petitions.

Response: Lord, hear our prayer.

For the church: may we seek greater unity with our Christian brothers and sisters around the world, we pray . . .

For leaders of nations: may collaboration for the common good and a commitment to protecting all citizens shape their governing, we pray . . .

For the sick and suffering: may their anxieties be relieved as they hope for healing, we pray . . .

For those in our midst experiencing divisions: may they seek and find reconciliation among family and friends, we pray . . .

Heavenly Father, you sent your Son so that we might come to know and believe in the love you have for us. Hear our prayers this day as we place our trust in you. We ask this through Christ our Lord. **Amen.**

Prayer

Spirit of God, you descend with power and fill hearts with courage and joy. Renew our faith, inspire our words, and unite us in love, that we may live boldly as your witnesses. May we bring hope, understanding, and the light of Christ into every corner of our world, homes, and hearts. **Amen.**

Gospel **John 20:19-23 (or John 15:26-27; 16:12-15) Mass during the Day**

On the evening of that first day of the week, when the doors were locked, where the disciples were, for fear of the Jews, Jesus came and stood in their midst and said to them, "Peace be with you." When he had said this, he showed them his hands and his side. The disciples rejoiced when they saw the Lord. Jesus said to them again, "Peace be with you. As the Father has sent me, so I send you." And when he had said this, he breathed on them and said to them, "Receive the Holy Spirit. Whose sins you forgive are forgiven them, and whose sins you retain are retained."

Brief Silence

For Reflection

Just before receiving the Spirit, those who have until then been hiding in the Upper Room are sent on a mission. The first specific directive is about the forgiveness of sins—or alternatively, the withholding of that forgiveness. This is the start of a new way of life for humanity. That new life begins with reconciliation, the healing of broken relationships, and the Holy Spirit empowers the disciples to extend resurrection life by offering forgiveness. Just as Jesus's resurrection overcomes death, the Spirit overcomes sin.

✦ Have you ever experienced Jesus showing up even when you didn't want someone else there?

Brief Silence

Model Universal Prayer (Prayer of the Faithful)

We come before the Lord who calls his faithful to pray for one another, as we pray . . .

Response: Lord, hear our prayer.

For the church on this holy day of Pentecost: may we shed our apathy and inaction and feel our hearts on fire with the Spirit, we pray . . .

For our leaders, and all called to watch over and protect their homelands: may the gifts of the Spirit guide them in the way of peace, we pray . . .

For those who are suffering, sick, lonely, and hopeless: may the Spirit of the Lord touch their lives through the people they encounter, we pray . . .

For all of us gathered here today: may no doors and no walls separate us from the love of Christ Jesus who stands in our midst, we pray . . .

Loving God, throughout time you have called your people to yourself. In these days you have given us your Holy Spirit to guide us ever more closely. Hear our prayers, and unite us in your Spirit through your Son. We ask this through Christ our Lord. **Amen.**

Prayer

Triune God, mystery of perfect love, you invite us into your eternal communion. Open our hearts to your presence and shape us by your wisdom. Guide us to live in harmony with one another, bearing witness to the joy and peace that flow from your boundless life. **Amen.**

Gospel **Matt 28:16-20**

The eleven disciples went to Galilee, to the mountain to which Jesus had ordered them. When they all saw him, they worshiped, but they doubted. Then Jesus approached and said to them, "All power in heaven and on earth has been given to me. Go, therefore, and make disciples of all nations, baptizing them in the name of the Father, and of the Son, and of the Holy Spirit, teaching them to observe all that I have commanded you. And behold, I am with you always, until the end of the age."

Brief Silence

For Reflection

Today's solemnity, in a way, could be seen as the "Solemnity of Who God Is, Not What God Does." Of course, what God has accomplished for us across salvation history is important, to dramatically understate things. We would be wise, however, to avoid naming God, especially the three persons, by titles of actions or accomplishments. We must rather recall that the persons of the Trinity are not defined by what they do, but only who they are: each God, related to but not the other two persons.

✦ What does the Trinity mean to you and for you? Does anything about it particularly strike you today?

Brief Silence

Model Universal Prayer (Prayer of the Faithful)

The Father, Son, and Holy Spirit are always for us and with us. Confident that our God is present, we bring to him our needs.

Response: Lord, hear our prayer.

For our bishops: may they convey the Trinity in their celebration of the sacraments and by opening the Scriptures, we pray . . .

For our elected officials: may they be informed by God's generous love so they might serve our nation with compassion and fidelity, we pray . . .

For the homeless and the hungry: may they find not only material shelter, but also the shelter of God's providence, we pray . . .

For the members of this parish, especially those who are sick: may they find accompaniment, community, and healing, we pray . . .

Triune God, you restore us to yourself by the gift of your covenant. We know that you are eternally ours and we ask that you hear our prayers with patience, mercy, and wisdom. We ask this through Christ our Lord. **Amen.**

THE MOST HOLY BODY AND BLOOD OF CHRIST (CORPUS CHRISTI)

Prayer

God of sustaining grace, in the Eucharist you dwell among us and strengthen our faith. Teach us to receive you with reverence. Let your presence transform our daily lives, and inspire us to become a living offering of love, compassion, and generosity in the world around us. **Amen.**

Gospel **Mark 14:12-16, 22-26**

On the first day of the Feast of Unleavened Bread, when they sacrificed the Passover lamb, Jesus' disciples said to him,"Where do you want us to go and prepare for you to eat the Passover?" He sent two of his disciples and said to them, "Go into the city and a man will meet you, carrying a jar of water. Follow him. Wherever he enters, say to the master of the house, 'The Teacher says, "Where is my guest room where I may eat the Passover with my disciples?"' Then he will show you a large upper room furnished and ready. Make the preparations for us there." The disciples then went off, entered the city, and found it just as he had told them; and they prepared the Passover.

While they were eating, he took bread, said the blessing, broke it, gave it to them, and said, "Take it; this is my body." Then he took a cup, gave thanks, and gave it to them, and they all drank from it. He said to them, "This is my blood of the covenant, which will be shed for many. Amen, I say to you, I shall not drink again the fruit of the vine until the day when I drink it new in the kingdom of God." Then, after singing a hymn, they went out to the Mount of Olives.

Brief Silence

For Reflection

Many of us are familiar with the expression "source and summit of our faith." This expression draws from the Vatican II Constitution on the Church, notably regarding the faithful: "Taking part in the Eucharistic sacrifice, the source and summit of the christian life, [the faithful] offer the divine victim to God and themselves along with him" (*Lumen Gentium* 11). This quote refers specifically to taking part in the eucharistic sacrifice—that is, the whole of Mass, not just the consumption of the host.

✦ Like Christ, how can you lay down your life for those who need you in a new way?

Brief Silence

Model Universal Prayer (Prayer of the Faithful)

Trusting that our God is truly for us, we approach him as we seek the well-being of the church and our world.

Response: Lord, hear our prayer.

For our Holy Father N.: that he might continue to gather the nations into Christ's body by his witness to the gospel, we pray . . .

For the leaders of nations: that they might heed the gospel's call for faith and repentance, we pray . . .

For the poorest members of Christ's body: that they might find healing, community, and peace and so find the wealth of our Lord, we pray . . .

For this parish: that its members might grow closer to one another by the observance of prayer and service, becoming more fully Christ's body for one another, we pray . . .

O God, you gather us into one by the saving body and blood of your Son, Christ Jesus. Confident in our union with him, we offer these petitions for the life of the world. We ask this through Christ our Lord. **Amen.**

Prayer

God of tender restoration, you bring life to places of emptiness and loss. Lead us to walk in your mercy and lift the spirits of the broken that our hearts may find courage and our actions reflect the quiet strength you awaken in us. **Amen.**

Gospel **Mark 3:20-35**

Jesus came home with his disciples. Again the crowd gathered, making it impossible for them even to eat. When his relatives heard of this they set out to seize him, for they said, "He is out of his mind." The scribes who had come from Jerusalem said, "He is possessed by Beelzebul," and "By the prince of demons he drives out demons."

Summoning them, he began to speak to them in parables, "How can Satan drive out Satan? If a kingdom is divided against itself, that kingdom cannot stand. And if a house is divided against itself, that house will not be able to stand. And if Satan has risen up against himself and is divided, he cannot stand; that is the end of him. But no one can enter a strong man's house to plunder his property unless he first ties up the strong man. Then he can plunder the house. Amen, I say to you, all sins and all blasphemies that people utter will be forgiven them. But whoever blasphemes against the Holy Spirit will never have forgiveness, but is guilty of an everlasting sin." For they had said, "He has an unclean spirit."

His mother and his brothers arrived. Standing outside they sent word to him and called him. A crowd seated around him told him, "Your mother and your brothers and your sisters are outside asking for you." But he said to them in reply, "Who are my mother and my brothers?" And looking around at those seated in the circle he said, "Here are my mother and my brothers. For whoever does the will of God is my brother and sister and mother."

Brief Silence

For Reflection

It's noteworthy that in this gospel, Jesus is redefining what it means to be family. Especially in our modern context, what constitutes a family continues to evolve, expand, and account for a myriad of circumstances. Jesus teaches that to him, family is "whoever does the will of God." Would that every parish family be bold enough to embrace that definition! No follower of Jesus is perfect, and this Sunday is a good time for each of us to check ourselves, both as individuals and as part of a Christian community.

✦ Do you love those who need you most? Are those people different from those with whom you are most familiar or comfortable?

Brief Silence

Model Universal Prayer (Prayer of the Faithful)

Trusting in the Lord who listens to our voice, we bring him our prayers and supplications for ourselves and all the world.

Response: Lord, hear our prayer.

For the church fed by the sacraments and led by the word: may we bring Christ's love to life in our works of charity and justice, we pray . . .

For those who lead, teach, and shape the lives of those around them: may they seek to bring about the glory of God in all they do, we pray . . .

For all who suffer from the violence of war and terror: may they find protection and peace in the mercy of Christ and the help of their neighbors, we pray . . .

For the church gathered here today: may we bring hope to those who are discouraged, we pray . . .

Lord God, you draw all people to yourself. As we lift our prayers to you, may we be raised with the Lord Jesus, and so always dwell in your presence. We ask this through Christ our Lord. **Amen.**

ELEVENTH SUNDAY IN ORDINARY TIME

Prayer

Lord of quiet wonder, you bring forth life in ways unseen. Open our eyes to the signs of your care, guide our hands to nurture what is fragile, and teach us to celebrate the small movements of grace that flourish into lasting joy. **Amen.**

Gospel **Mark 4:26-34**

Jesus said to the crowds: "This is how it is with the kingdom of God; it is as if a man were to scatter seed on the land and would sleep and rise night and day and through it all the seed would sprout and grow, he knows not how. Of its own accord the land yields fruit, first the blade, then the ear, then the full grain in the ear. And when the grain is ripe, he wields the sickle at once, for the harvest has come."

He said, "To what shall we compare the kingdom of God, or what parable can we use for it? It is like a mustard seed that, when it is sown in the ground, is the smallest of all the seeds on the earth. But once it is sown, it springs up and becomes the largest of plants and puts forth large branches, so that the birds of the sky can dwell in its shade." With many such parables he spoke the word to them as they were able to understand it. Without parables he did not speak to them, but to his own disciples he explained everything in private.

Brief Silence

For Reflection

The mustard seed in Jesus's parable today is small, unassuming, and ordinary. Yet God can take the ordinary and from it, if hearts are receptive and willing, bring about holiness, devotion, and even saintliness. Consider the posture of sitting. It may not look like action or power, but it is the posture of growth—the fertile stillness where something begins to take root. Just as the mustard seed holds potential for astonishing growth, sitting attentively before the Word allows the seed of faith to be planted and nurtured in us.

✦ Of the images Jesus uses to explain the kingdom of God, which connects with you most readily?

Brief Silence

Model Universal Prayer (Prayer of the Faithful)

Gathering our prayers and petitions, we offer them before the Lord who comes to dwell in our midst.

Response: Lord, hear our prayer.

For the church, scattered throughout the world: may the word of God take root in the hearts of young people and fill them with zeal for their faith, we pray . . .

For nations struggling against the powers of corruption: may their leaders be filled with courage to withstand political pressures and to protect their people, we pray . . .

For all those suffering in mind, body, and spirit: may they take strength and courage in the Lord's mercy, and find healing at the hands of their caregivers, we pray . . .

For all gathered here this day: may we remember our mission to go forth and witness to the love of Christ through our daily lives, we pray . . .

Loving God, you gather all people to yourself. Hear our prayers this day and allow us who have heard your word to share the joy of the gospel throughout the earth. We ask this through Christ our Lord. **Amen.**

TWELFTH SUNDAY IN ORDINARY TIME

Prayer

God of steadfast courage, you watch over us in the storms of life. Give us trust in your guidance and hearts untroubled by fear that we may stand firm and move forward with confidence in your faithful care. **Amen.**

Gospel **Mark 4:35-41**

On that day, as evening drew on, Jesus said to his disciples: "Let us cross to the other side." Leaving the crowd, they took Jesus with them in the boat just as he was. And other boats were with him. A violent squall came up and waves were breaking over the boat, so that it was already filling up. Jesus was in the stern, asleep on a cushion. They woke him and said to him, "Teacher, do you not care that we are perishing?" He woke up, rebuked the wind, and said to the sea, " Quiet! Be still!" The wind ceased and there was great calm. Then he asked them, "Why are you terrified? Do you not yet have faith?" They were filled with great awe and said to one another, "Who then is this whom even wind and sea obey?"

Brief Silence

For Reflection

Very few of us experience God in such an obvious, tangible way as do the disciples in today's gospel. Inasmuch as we might experience individually God's voice in communal prayer, the whole of the community also experiences God: Christ sharing himself by his presence in word, Eucharist, the priest-celebrant, and the assembly itself. The answer to our prayers at liturgy then, whatever they are, is always relationship with God (word, sacrifice, meal) and with one another (priest and assembly), all underpinned by faith and trust.

✦ Can Jesus's command to "be still" bring peace to some part of your life today? Where do you most need stillness?

Brief Silence

Model Universal Prayer (Prayer of the Faithful)

The Lord hears our distress and our every need. We bring our prayers and petitions before him, trusting in his providence and care.

Response: Lord, hear our prayer.

For the church: may we have greater courage to speak and be God's justice and mercy despite the tumult of the world around us, we pray . . .

For all who serve as leaders in their family, their workplaces, or their communities: may they have the wisdom to offer direction to those who rely upon them, we pray . . .

For those suffering from oppression and violence within their homes: may peace and protection come quickly, we pray . . .

For us who are gathered here today: may the love of Christ compel us to love those who surround us, we pray . . .

God our Father, just as you ordered the cosmos from chaos into creation, you dispel sin from our lives with your great love. Hear our prayers this day as we long for peace throughout our world. We ask this through Christ our Lord. **Amen.**

THE NATIVITY OF SAINT JOHN THE BAPTIST

Prayer

Lord of steadfast purpose, you raised John to herald your saving plan. Guide us to recognize your work in our lives and inspire us to follow your call with clarity, boldness, and joy as we bear witness to your goodness in our world. **Amen.**

Gospel **Luke 1:57-66, 80 (or Luke 1:5-17, Vigil Mass)**

When the time arrived for Elizabeth to have her child she gave birth to a son. Her neighbors and relatives heard that the Lord had shown his great mercy toward her, and they rejoiced with her. When they came on the eighth day to circumcise the child, they were going to call him Zechariah after his father, but his mother said in reply, "No. He will be called John." But they answered her, "There is no one among your relatives who has this name." So they made signs, asking his father what he wished him to be called. He asked for a tablet and wrote, "John is his name," and all were amazed. Immediately his mouth was opened, his tongue freed, and he spoke blessing God. Then fear came upon all their neighbors, and all these matters were discussed throughout the hill country of Judea. All who heard these things took them to heart, saying, "What, then, will this child be?" For surely the hand of the Lord was with him.

The child grew and became strong in spirit, and he was in the desert until the day of his manifestation to Israel.

Brief Silence

For Reflection

In today's gospel, everyone is astounded that Elizabeth and Zechariah would name their child John, as it wasn't a name in their family history. Proclaiming "John is his name" in writing is what finally allows Zechariah to regain his speaking voice. It is important that each member of our Christian community know one another by name. This is a first and elemental sign that you care about them and hope to know them better. It's recognizing that the Body of Christ is incomplete if just one person is absent, unknown.

✦ How is Eucharist and receiving Communion, whether at church or while homebound or in a health facility, an act of really knowing one another?

Brief Silence

Model Universal Prayer (Prayer of the Faithful)

Coming before the Lord who is ever faithful, we offer our prayers and petitions.

Response: Lord, hear our prayer.

That all who are baptized might find renewed hope and strengthened faith this day, we pray . . .

That our leaders, managers, and all who hold authority will take time to listen to the needs of those they serve, we pray . . .

That all who long for the birth of a child might find reason for joy, we pray . . .

That we may remember and value our loved ones who are among us and who are far from us, we pray . . .

Loving God, you gave your faithful servants, Zechariah and Elizabeth, their child, John. Increase our faith, so that we might live with joyful hope in the life of your Son, Jesus Christ, who lives and reigns with you in the unity of the Holy Spirit, God forever and ever. **Amen.**

THIRTEENTH SUNDAY IN ORDINARY TIME

Prayer

God who draws all people to newness of life, you invite us to follow your Son in all things. Give us the courage to let go of what holds us back and the strength to walk faithfully in the path of service and devotion you set before us. **Amen.**

Gospel **Mark 5:21-43 (or Mark 5:21-24, 35b-43)**

When Jesus had crossed again in the boat to the other side, a large crowd gathered around him, and he stayed close to the sea. One of the synagogue officials, named Jairus, came forward. Seeing him he fell at his feet and pleaded earnestly with him, saying, "My daughter is at the point of death. Please, come lay your hands on her that she may get well and live." He went off with him, and a large crowd followed him and pressed upon him.

There was a woman afflicted with hemorrhages for twelve years. She had suffered greatly at the hands of many doctors and had spent all that she had. Yet she was not helped but only grew worse. She had heard about Jesus and came up behind him in the crowd and touched his cloak. She said, "If I but touch his clothes, I shall be cured." Immediately her flow of blood dried up. She felt in her body that she was healed of her affliction. Jesus, aware at once that power had gone out from him, turned around in the crowd and asked, "Who has touched my clothes?" But his disciples said to Jesus, "You see how the crowd is pressing upon you, and yet you ask, 'Who touched me?'" And he looked around to see who had done it. The woman, realizing what had happened to her, approached in fear and trembling. She fell down before Jesus and told him the whole truth. He said to her, "Daughter, your faith has saved you. Go in peace and be cured of your affliction."

While he was still speaking, people from the synagogue official's house arrived and said, "Your daughter has died; why trouble the teacher any longer?" Disregarding the message that was reported, Jesus said to the synagogue official, "Do not be afraid; just have faith." He did not allow anyone to accompany him inside except Peter, James, and John, the brother of James. When they arrived at the house of the synagogue official, he caught sight of a commotion, people weeping and wailing loudly. So he went in and said to them, "Why this commotion and weeping? The child is not dead but asleep." And they ridiculed him. Then he put them all out. He took along the child's father and mother and those who were with him and entered the room where the child was. He took the child by the hand and said to her, *"Talitha koum,"* which means, "Little girl, I say to you, arise!" The girl, a child of twelve, arose immediately and walked around. At that they were utterly astounded. He gave strict orders that no one should know this and said that she should be given something to eat.

Brief Silence

For Reflection

There are very few Aramaic words of Jesus quoted directly in Scripture. So when we do encounter them—like *"Talitha koum,"* spoken to Jairus's daughter—we should recognize their deep importance. In our call to share the good news with others, the words we choose are of utmost importance, and we must consider what we wish the response to be. We must approach each person with specific care and attention, that our kerygma elicit in them the new life that Jesus's *"Talitha koum"* did of Jairus's daughter.

✦ Like the father of the little girl, how can you reach out to Christ on behalf of someone else who needs healing?

THIRTEENTH SUNDAY IN ORDINARY TIME

Brief Silence

Model Universal Prayer (Prayer of the Faithful)

Coming before the Lord who is always our helper, we offer our prayers and petitions.

Response: Lord, hear our prayer.

For Pope N., our Bishop N., and all our priests and deacons: may they be filled with the grace and truth of our Lord Jesus Christ, we pray . . .

For leaders of nations facing the effects of climate change: may their partnership and dialogue find solutions for their people and their futures, we pray . . .

For all who lack resources to sustain their families: may those blessed with abundance be filled with generosity toward those in need, we pray . . .

For us gathered here today to celebrate these sacred mysteries: may we find rich fare in the word of God proclaimed, we pray . . .

Loving God, your Son, Jesus Christ, destroyed death and brought new hope to life through the gospel. Hear our prayers this day, and draw us closer to you as we seek to make his gospel known throughout the world. We ask this through Christ our Lord. **Amen.**

FOURTEENTH SUNDAY IN ORDINARY TIME

Prayer

Jesus, gentle Teacher, you invite us to lay down our burdens and find rest in your care. Open our hearts to your guidance and help us receive your peace that our spirits may be renewed and our lives shaped by your wisdom. **Amen.**

Gospel **Mark 6:1-6**

Jesus departed from there and came to his native place, accompanied by his disciples. When the sabbath came he began to teach in the synagogue, and many who heard him were astonished. They said, "Where did this man get all this? What kind of wisdom has been given him? What mighty deeds are wrought by his hands! Is he not the carpenter, the son of Mary, and the brother of James and Joses and Judas and Simon? And are not his sisters here with us?" And they took offense at him. Jesus said to them, "A prophet is not without honor except in his native place and among his own kin and in his own house." So he was not able to perform any mighty deed there, apart from curing a few sick people by laying his hands on them. He was amazed at their lack of faith.

Brief Silence

For Reflection

Communication always carries risk. No matter the medium—spoken, written, or digital—listeners and readers interpret through their own lens, drawing from tone, context, or cultural background, often mishearing or misunderstanding, even when intentions are good. Perhaps this is a main reason that even Jesus was received in his native place—as we hear in today's gospel—without honor. On civic holidays like today, we must be mindful of the universal nature of the church and the diverse people gathered in Christ's name in how we communicate with each other.

✦ Have you ever failed to see that God was in your midst? When and why so?

Brief Silence

Model Universal Prayer (Prayer of the Faithful)

Relying on the Lord's grace, let us offer our prayers for those in need.

Response: Lord, hear our prayer.

For the church scattered throughout the world: may the faithful experience grace and hope, especially in communities suffering from persecution, we pray . . .

For leaders of nations: may they be acutely attentive to the suffering in their midst, we pray . . .

For those who have become refugees due to natural disasters: may they be granted safety and swift return to their homes, we pray . . .

For all who love God, especially amidst our local communities: may the love of God feed our love of our neighbors, we pray . . .

Loving God, you sent your Spirit out into the world so that we might hear your voice and respond to your call. Hear our prayers this day and allow us to be agents of your love. We ask this through Christ our Lord. **Amen.**

FIFTEENTH SUNDAY IN ORDINARY TIME

Prayer

God of abundant harvest, you scatter your word with care and patience. Help us to receive it with open hearts and nurture its growth so that our actions may bear fruit in kindness, generosity, and faithfulness to your call. **Amen.**

Gospel **Mark 6:7-13**

Jesus summoned the Twelve and began to send them out two by two and gave them authority over unclean spirits. He instructed them to take nothing for the journey but a walking stick—no food, no sack, no money in their belts. They were, however, to wear sandals but not a second tunic. He said to them, "Wherever you enter a house, stay there until you leave. Whatever place does not welcome you or listen to you, leave there and shake the dust off your feet in testimony against them." So they went off and preached repentance. The Twelve drove out many demons, and they anointed with oil many who were sick and cured them.

Brief Silence

For Reflection

Jesus sends his apostles to proclaim the reign of God. He tells them to stay once they have entered a house through which one must pass through the door. The door to the church is a gateway to heaven itself, or at least a foretaste of it. Candidates in OCIA are met at those doors, as is a casket, holding the remains of a loved one. As we enter the church by such a door we too are sent out to be Christ's hands and feet in the world.

✦ Have you ever chosen to commit or recommit to others, even those who were difficult, because you knew that God was calling you to care for them? How did you know to do so?

Brief Silence

Model Universal Prayer (Prayer of the Faithful)

Coming before the Lord, we place our hope in him as we offer our prayers and petitions.

Response: Lord, hear our prayer.

For the church throughout the world: may the faithful find confidence in Christ in the midst of secularism and worldly powers, we pray . . .

For those who teach, who minister, and who serve in missions: may they find courage in their work and support in their communities, we pray . . .

For all who do not believe in God: may their spirits be moved by the witness of the faithful and their hearts awakened by God's love, we pray . . .

For us gathered here: may we always welcome the stranger in our midst, treating visitors and newcomers with graciousness and dignity, we pray . . .

Lord God, we seek always to follow you with our whole self. May our hearts, our minds, and our strength be devoted to your love and to the care of our neighbor. We ask this through Christ our Lord. **Amen.**

SIXTEENTH SUNDAY IN ORDINARY TIME

Prayer

God of steadfast watchfulness, you gather the lost and tend the weary. Teach us to follow your voice with trust and to extend your patience and reassurance to all we encounter so that your goodness may flourish through our deeds. **Amen.**

Gospel **Mark 6:30-34**

The apostles gathered together with Jesus and reported all they had done and taught. He said to them, "Come away by yourselves to a deserted place and rest a while." People were coming and going in great numbers, and they had no opportunity even to eat. So they went off in the boat by themselves to a deserted place. People saw them leaving and many came to know about it. They hastened there on foot from all the towns and arrived at the place before them.

When he disembarked and saw the vast crowd, his heart was moved with pity for them, for they were like sheep without a shepherd; and he began to teach them many things.

Brief Silence

For Reflection

In the gospel today, Jesus invites the apostles to "Come away by yourselves." Forming smaller Christian communities within a larger whole has immense value in this regard. Small, faith-sharing groups intensify a sense of belonging in a world where the number of close friendships is shrinking, and people yearn for any connection and "fitting in." We can also do our part to make every liturgy a place where all feel welcome, valued, and engaged. Thus, the whole community can grow together in holiness and unity.

✦ Have you ever been afraid to step away from those who surround you, in order to rest and pray? How can you do so in a way that is still generous and loving?

Brief Silence

Model Universal Prayer (Prayer of the Faithful)

We come before the Lord who always hears his people as we offer our prayers and petitions.

Response: Lord, hear our prayer.

For the church, especially all who have suffered from the crisis of abuse: may healing, protection, and the Lord's mercy and justice guide the faithful always, we pray . . .

For our bishops throughout the world: may they exhort the faithful to follow Christ Jesus and to find peace with one another, we pray . . .

For those who walk in the darkness of the valley of death: may they fear no evil, and know the presence of the Lord, we pray . . .

For those of us gathered here today: may we allow the Good Shepherd to guide us and to fill our hearts with the food from his table, we pray . . .

O God, you sent your Son to call us to yourself. Grant that we might hear your voice this day, and heed your call to follow you in justice and righteousness. We ask this through Christ our Lord. **Amen.**

SEVENTEENTH SUNDAY IN ORDINARY TIME

Prayer

God of daily provision, you sustain us with the gifts we need. Teach us to rely on your care and share generously with others that we may experience the abundance of your goodness in our lives and in the lives of those around us. **Amen.**

Gospel **John 6:1-15**

Jesus went across the Sea of Galilee. A large crowd followed him, because they saw the signs he was performing on the sick. Jesus went up on the mountain, and there he sat down with his disciples. The Jewish feast of Passover was near. When Jesus raised his eyes and saw that a large crowd was coming to him, he said to Philip, "Where can we buy enough food for them to eat?" He said this to test him, because he himself knew what he was going to do. Philip answered him, "Two hundred days' wages worth of food would not be enough for each of them to have a little." One of his disciples, Andrew, the brother of Simon Peter, said to him, "There is a boy here who has five barley loaves and two fish; but what good are these for so many?" Jesus said, "Have the people recline." Now there was a great deal of grass in that place. So the men reclined, about five thousand in number. Then Jesus took the loaves, gave thanks, and distributed them to those who were reclining, and also as much of the fish as they wanted. When they had had their fill, he said to his disciples, "Gather the fragments left over, so that nothing will be wasted." So they collected them, and filled twelve wicker baskets with fragments from the five barley loaves that had been more than they could eat. When the people saw the sign he had done, they said, "This is truly the Prophet, the one who is to come into the world." Since Jesus knew that they were going to come and carry him off to make him king, he withdrew again to the mountain alone.

Brief Silence

For Reflection

It is seemingly no accident that in our rites the assembly is sent forth almost immediately upon reception of the Eucharist. Within mere moments, the presider pronounces the dismissal: "*Ite, missa est*"—which roughly translates to "Go, you are sent." "Go" is what we're told, not "but wait, adore for a minute what is literally now inside you." Our mission work as faithful disciples, the Christian activity we are all called to, begins immediately while we are still literally filled with Christ's Real Presence, which a waiting world sorely needs.

✦ Has God ever exceeded your expectations? What does that say to you about God? About yourself?

Brief Silence

Model Universal Prayer (Prayer of the Faithful)

The hand of the Lord feeds us; he answers all our needs. Trusting in him, let us come before the Lord with our prayers and petitions.

Response: Lord, hear our prayer.

For the church, and for Christians throughout the world: may we one day grow closer in communion, and work side by side in charity for the world as we wait, we pray . . .

For our leaders here and throughout our nation: may they support initiatives for sustainable agriculture, and the protection of those who grow and cultivate our food, we pray . . .

For those imprisoned unjustly: may they find release and freedom, and untiring support from their friends, we pray . . .

For all gathered here today: may prejudice be stripped from our hearts, we pray . . .

O God, you call us to one faith, one baptism, and one hope. Draw us ever closer to Jesus Christ your Son, so that we might all be one in him. We ask this through Christ our Lord. **Amen.**

EIGHTEENTH SUNDAY IN ORDINARY TIME

Prayer

Lord of true abundance, you show us that the riches of heaven surpass those of earth. Open our eyes to the treasures of faith and generosity and inspire us to live simply and share freely so that your goodness may flourish in every heart. **Amen.**

Gospel **John 6:24-35**

When the crowd saw that neither Jesus nor his disciples were there, they themselves got into boats and came to Capernaum looking for Jesus. And when they found him across the sea they said to him, "Rabbi, when did you get here?" Jesus answered them and said, "Amen, amen, I say to you, you are looking for me not because you saw signs but because you ate the loaves and were filled. Do not work for food that perishes but for the food that endures for eternal life, which the Son of Man will give you. For on him the Father, God, has set his seal." So they said to him, "What can we do to accomplish the works of God?" Jesus answered and said to them, "This is the work of God, that you believe in the one he sent." So they said to him, "What sign can you do, that we may see and believe in you? What can you do? Our ancestors ate manna in the desert, as it is written: / *He gave them bread from heaven to eat.*" / So Jesus said to them, "Amen, amen, I say to you, it was not Moses who gave the bread from heaven; my Father gives you the true bread from heaven. For the bread of God is that which comes down from heaven and gives life to the world."

So they said to him, "Sir, give us this bread always." Jesus said to them, "I am the bread of life; whoever comes to me will never hunger, and whoever believes in me will never thirst."

Brief Silence

For Reflection

The theme of today's readings is one of dependence, relying on God completely for sustenance. This is elaborated in the words of the Lord's Prayer: "Give us this day our daily bread." This prayer asks for only what is needed today and petitions the Lord to provide it. This complete dependence is something most of us are not well versed in or willing to accept. Dependence isn't something that can be faked. It must be lived by example, by prayer into action, or even inaction, if you will.

✦ Do you struggle to believe Jesus's words? What about him is hardest for you to believe at this moment?

Brief Silence

Model Universal Prayer (Prayer of the Faithful)

We turn to the Lord who gives forth words of life, offering our prayers for ourselves and all the world.

Response: Lord, hear our prayer.

For the church: may the faithful throughout the world draw more deeply from the life of the Eucharist, finding nourishment that sustains them, we pray . . .

For leaders in our communities, our cities, and our nation: may they not succumb to corruption through deceitful desires, but follow God's ways of righteousness and truth, we pray . . .

For refugees and migrants: may they find safe passage in their journeys and new life in their destinations, we pray . . .

For those of us gathered here today: may our fears and anxieties be released by the Lord who reigns over all, we pray . . .

Lord God, you fill your people with good things and feed us with abundance. Hear our prayers this day as we hope for all the world to be filled with your goodness and truth. We ask this through Christ our Lord. **Amen.**

NINETEENTH SUNDAY IN ORDINARY TIME

Prayer

Lord of quiet strength, you invite us to trust when storms surround us. Help us to rely on your word and presence and inspire confidence in our hearts so that our steps may reflect your steady hand and your unwavering commitment to our lives. **Amen.**

Gospel **John 6:41-51**

The Jews murmured about Jesus because he said, "I am the bread that came down from heaven," and they said, "Is this not Jesus, the son of Joseph? Do we not know his father and mother? Then how can he say, 'I have come down from heaven'?" Jesus answered and said to them, "Stop murmuring among yourselves. No one can come to me unless the Father who sent me draw him, and I will raise him on the last day. It is written in the prophets: / *They shall all be taught by God.* / Everyone who listens to my Father and learns from him comes to me. Not that anyone has seen the Father except the one who is from God; he has seen the Father. Amen, amen, I say to you, whoever believes has eternal life. I am the bread of life. Your ancestors ate the manna in the desert, but they died; this is the bread that comes down from heaven so that one may eat it and not die. I am the living bread that came down from heaven; whoever eats this bread will live forever; and the bread that I will give is my flesh for the life of the world."

Brief Silence

For Reflection

In the gospel today, we can note the emphasis on the Bread of Life sustaining us, and in a way different than other foods—like the manna we pondered a week ago. This bread not only sustains us physically until tomorrow, but "whoever eats this bread will live forever." Some choose to attend Mass daily to partake in such sustenance. Whether daily or only on Sundays, the church's liturgy is our prescribed, corporate prayer; the liturgy is our source and summit, our opportunity to partake in the Bread of Life.

✦ Jesus is food for life, but what kind of nourishment do you most need from him today? Where do you need refreshment?

Brief Silence

Model Universal Prayer (Prayer of the Faithful)

God our Father listens to his children who come to him. Let us approach him now with our prayers and petitions for ourselves and all the world.

Response: Lord, hear our prayer.

For the faithful throughout the world: may they find food for their spirits at the table of God's word and the table of the Eucharist, we pray . . .

For our leaders: may they reject bitter rhetoric that clenches hearts, responding to the needs of their people with compassion and patience, we pray . . .

For all who lack access to adequate food and to healthy food: may those blessed with abundance recognize their need, we pray . . .

For the faithful gathered here: may we practice compassion with those closest to us, especially our parents, spouses, children, and families, we pray . . .

O God, you have prepared your people for your kingdom with the seal of baptism. Hear us in our need and draw us closer to you as your faithful children. We ask this through Christ our Lord. **Amen.**

THE ASSUMPTION OF THE BLESSED VIRGIN MARY

Prayer

God of wondrous triumph, you raised Mary, full of grace, into the glory of heaven. Guide us to follow her example of faithful discipleship and open our hearts to your call so that we may live with hope, joy, and steadfast devotion to your ways. **Amen.**

Gospel **Luke 1:39-56, Mass during the Day (or Luke 11:27-28, Vigil Mass)**

Mary set out and traveled to the hill country in haste to a town of Judah, where she entered the house of Zechariah and greeted Elizabeth. When Elizabeth heard Mary's greeting, the infant leaped in her womb, and Elizabeth, filled with the Holy Spirit, cried out in a loud voice and said, "Blessed are you among women, and blessed is the fruit of your womb. And how does this happen to me, that the mother of my Lord should come to me? For at the moment the sound of your greeting reached my ears, the infant in my womb leaped for joy. Blessed are you who believed that what was spoken to you by the Lord would be fulfilled."

And Mary said: / "My soul proclaims the greatness of the Lord; / my spirit rejoices in God my Savior / for he has looked with favor on his lowly servant. / From this day all generations will call me blessed: / the Almighty has done great things for me, / and holy is his Name. / He has mercy on those who fear him / in every generation. / He has shown the strength of his arm, / and has scattered the proud in their conceit. / He has cast down the mighty from their thrones, / and has lifted up the lowly. / He has filled the hungry with good things, / and the rich he has sent away empty. / He has come to the help of his servant Israel / for he has remembered his promise of mercy, / the promise he made to our fathers, / to Abraham and his children forever."

Mary remained with her about three months and then returned to her home.

Brief Silence

For Reflection

On the solemnity of the Assumption, we encounter the *Magnificat* (Luke 1:46-55), Mary's own canticle of praise. Her words are deeply Christocentric, proclaiming the greatness of God, his mercy, and his justice. In singing Mary's song, the church echoes not just her devotion but her prophetic joy in the saving power of God. The *Magnificat* isn't only Mary's hymn, it is ours as well. Far from detracting from the eucharistic celebration, the *Magnificat* can focus us more fully on the mystery of Christ's presence, as Mary herself always does.

✦ How well do you feel you know Mary? Can you read more about her? Can you pray with Mary?

Brief Silence

Model Universal Prayer (Prayer of the Faithful)

Turning in trust to the Lord who hears all our needs, we offer our prayers this day.

Response: Lord, hear our prayer.

For the church: with Mary, may we offer hope for the hopeless and lift up all who are bowed down, we pray . . .

For all those in power: may they use their might to fill the hungry with good things, we pray . . .

For those longing for guidance in their lives: may they feel the prompting and direction of the Spirit in their prayer, we pray . . .

For all of us gathered here today: may we recognize those who need encouragement, kindness, or patience, and find the courage to offer it, we pray . . .

O God, your servant, Mary, full of grace, responded to your word with joyful hope. Increase our faith, free us from our fears, and fill us with the fire of your love. We ask this through Christ our Lord. **Amen.**

TWENTY-FIRST SUNDAY IN ORDINARY TIME

Prayer

Christ our cornerstone, you invite us to stand firm in faith and embrace your word. Inspire us to shape our choices by his example and walk with confidence so that our lives may shine with your care and bear witness to your presence in every moment. **Amen.**

Gospel **John 6:60-69**

Many of Jesus' disciples who were listening said, "This saying is hard; who can accept it?" Since Jesus knew that his disciples were murmuring about this, he said to them, "Does this shock you? What if you were to see the Son of Man ascending to where he was before? It is the spirit that gives life, while the flesh is of no avail. The words I have spoken to you are Spirit and life. But there are some of you who do not believe." Jesus knew from the beginning the ones who would not believe and the one who would betray him. And he said, "For this reason I have told you that no one can come to me unless it is granted him by my Father."

As a result of this, many of his disciples returned to their former way of life and no longer accompanied him. Jesus then said to the Twelve, "Do you also want to leave?" Simon Peter answered him, "Master, to whom shall we go? You have the words of eternal life. We have come to believe and are convinced that you are the Holy One of God."

Brief Silence

For Reflection

In the preceding verses to this week's gospel, Jesus tells the quarreling crowd, "Unless you eat the flesh of the Son of Man and drink his blood, you do not have life within you"

(John 6:53). This shocking catechesis sets up today's passage, the conclusion of our weeks-long retreat on Jesus, the Bread of Life. Today's readings present our response to Christ's difficult teachings and the abundance, reliance, sustenance, and union given to us: belief. "Master, to whom shall we go? You have the words of eternal life."

✦ Have you ever wanted to walk away from someone who disagreed with you? Was there something you learned from their disagreement?

Brief Silence

Model Universal Prayer (Prayer of the Faithful)

The Lord hears the cries of the just and remains close to the brokenhearted. Let us remember to trust in the Lord, bringing before him our prayers and petitions.

Response: Lord, hear our prayer.

For the faithful throughout the world, especially those undergoing persecution: may they find safety in their distress and hope for their future, we pray . . .

For families throughout the world: may the value of the smallest human communities be preserved and protected, we pray . . .

For husbands and wives experiencing hardship in their relationships and in their lives: may they find counsel and hope, we pray . . .

For all of us gathered here today: may we choose always to serve the Lord through our words, our actions, and our love for one another, we pray . . .

O God, you call us to serve you without ceasing. Fill us with fortitude and strength to always follow your will and to encourage all around us to live in your love. We ask this through Christ our Lord. **Amen.**

TWENTY-SECOND SUNDAY IN ORDINARY TIME

Prayer

Lord of hidden treasures, you delight in hearts that seek truth and simplicity. Teach us to release pride and pretense and embrace your ways with humility so that our words and deeds may reflect your care and bring peace and renewal to all we encounter. **Amen.**

Gospel **Mark 7:1-8, 14-15, 21-23**

When the Pharisees with some scribes who had come from Jerusalem gathered around Jesus, they observed that some of his disciples ate their meals with unclean, that is, unwashed, hands.—For the Pharisees and, in fact, all Jews, do not eat without carefully washing their hands, keeping the tradition of the elders. And on coming from the marketplace they do not eat without purifying themselves. And there are many other things that they have traditionally observed, the purification of cups and jugs and kettles and beds.—So the Pharisees and scribes questioned him, "Why do your disciples not follow the tradition of the elders but instead eat a meal with unclean hands?" He responded, "Well did Isaiah prophesy about you hypocrites, as it is written: / *This people honors me with their lips, / but their hearts are far from me; / in vain do they worship me, / teaching as doctrines human precepts.* / You disregard God's commandment but cling to human tradition."

He summoned the crowd again and said to them, "Hear me, all of you, and understand. Nothing that enters one from outside can defile that person; but the things that come out from within are what defile.

"From within people, from their hearts, come evil thoughts, unchastity, theft, murder, adultery, greed, malice, deceit, licentiousness, envy, blasphemy, arrogance, folly. All these evils come from within and they defile."

Brief Silence

For Reflection

If those with whom we hope to share the good news don't know us and trust us as friends, any words we share will be hollow and distrusted. If those with whom we hope to share the good news are hungry, poorly clothed, or need shelter, these basic human needs will preclude them from hearing any other message. It's likely that the "needs" of those many of us meet are not needs relating to hunger or housing insecurity, but rather needs of relationship: belonging, being understood, sensing one's own belonging.

✦ Do you spend too much time on appearance, on outer things that do not matter? How can you, like Christ advises, work on the purity of what is inside you?

Brief Silence

Model Universal Prayer (Prayer of the Faithful)

Humbly coming before the Lord who calls all to holiness, we offer our prayers and petitions.

Response: Lord, hear our prayer.

That the faithful support one another in solidarity and unceasingly defend the human dignity of all, we pray . . .

That nations acting with aggression might be transformed by peace, and those they are persecuting be protected, we pray . . .

That the poor and vulnerable who have been forced to pay bribes for their protection may find new freedom from fear, we pray . . .

That we might allow the wisdom of God to enlighten our hearts and minds as we seek always to do God's will, we pray . . .

Lord God, you call us to be not only hearers but doers of the word. May we welcome your word always and live fully in your presence. We ask this through Christ our Lord. **Amen.**

TWENTY-THIRD SUNDAY IN ORDINARY TIME

Prayer

Lord of restoration, you make the wounded whole and the weary strong. Guide us to offer forgiveness and care with patience and understanding so that our words and actions may reflect your love and draw others into the wholeness you desire for all. **Amen.**

Gospel **Mark 7:31-37**

Again Jesus left the district of Tyre and went by way of Sidon to the Sea of Galilee, into the district of the Decapolis. And people brought to him a deaf man who had a speech impediment and begged him to lay his hand on him. He took him off by himself away from the crowd. He put his finger into the man's ears and, spitting, touched his tongue; then he looked up to heaven and groaned, and said to him, *"Ephphatha!"*—that is, "Be opened! "—And immediately the man's ears were opened, his speech impediment was removed, and he spoke plainly. He ordered them not to tell anyone. But the more he ordered them not to, the more they proclaimed it. They were exceedingly astonished and they said, "He has done all things well. He makes the deaf hear and the mute speak."

Brief Silence

For Reflection

Today's gospel, as did one earlier this year, includes Aramaic words: *"Ephphatha!"* "Be opened!" The church continues to wrestle with questions of openness, especially around the Eucharist. Pope Francis, in *Evangelii Gaudium* (The Joy of the Gospel), reminded us that the Eucharist is "not a prize for the perfect but a powerful medicine and nourishment for the weak" (EG 47). Let us be vigilant in being open to all who seek Christ—especially in the liturgy—without placing artificial restrictions on who may pray, serve, or be nourished by grace.

✦ Can Christ, who opens ears, mouths, and hearts, open something new for you this week?

Brief Silence

Model Universal Prayer (Prayer of the Faithful)

Coming before the Lord who heals the oppressed and sustains those who are broken in body and spirit, we offer our prayers and petitions.

Response: Lord, hear our prayer.

For the church: may the faithful throughout the world work for the protection and care of the most vulnerable in our midst, we pray . . .

For nations experiencing drought, heat, torrential rain, and excessive cold: may the suffering find relief, and may communities find long-term solutions, we pray . . .

For all those struggling with pain, weakness, and fatigue: may they find relief for their bodies and sustenance for their spirits, we pray . . .

For all of us gathered here today: may we remember to care for our bodies as well as our souls, pursuing healthy habits and lifestyles, we pray . . .

O God, you give life to all creation and sustain it in your love. Hear our prayers this day, and may we find healing and hope in your sustaining care. We ask this through Christ, our Lord. **Amen.**

TWENTY-FOURTH SUNDAY IN ORDINARY TIME

Prayer

Lord of reconciliation, show us the path of forgiveness and invite us to release all resentment. Help us to mend relationships and live with hearts open to grace so that your love flows through us and touches everyone around us. **Amen.**

Gospel **Mark 8:27-35**

Jesus and his disciples set out for the villages of Caesarea Philippi. Along the way he asked his disciples, "Who do people say that I am?" They said in reply, "John the Baptist, others Elijah, still others one of the prophets." And he asked them, "But who do you say that I am?" Peter said to him in reply, "You are the Christ." Then he warned them not to tell anyone about him.

He began to teach them that the Son of Man must suffer greatly and be rejected by the elders, the chief priests, and the scribes, and be killed, and rise after three days. He spoke this openly. Then Peter took him aside and began to rebuke him. At this he turned around and, looking at his disciples, rebuked Peter and said, "Get behind me, Satan. You are thinking not as God does, but as human beings do."

He summoned the crowd with his disciples and said to them, "Whoever wishes to come after me must deny himself, take up his cross, and follow me. For whoever wishes to save his life will lose it, but whoever loses his life for my sake and that of the gospel will save it."

Brief Silence

For Reflection

Jesus asks his disciples, "But who do you say that I am?" We might imagine a parallel question from Christ: "Where do you say that I am?" While Christ is not bound by time or space, the Vatican II Constitution on the Sacred Liturgy teaches that Christ is truly present in the liturgy in four ways: in the assembly, the word, the presiding minister, and uniquely so in the Eucharist. So when we gather around the altar, Christ is in our midst: in each other, in the altar, and in the Eucharist we share.

✦ How can you embrace the mystery of Christ's suffering with new joy and wisdom today?

Brief Silence

Model Universal Prayer (Prayer of the Faithful)

The Lord calls us to follow him in love and justice. Having heard his word, we begin by offering our prayers for the world.

Response: Lord, hear our prayer.

That all Christians who are persecuted, especially among our Eastern Orthodox brothers and sisters, find mercy and refuge, we pray . . .

That we might work to support the most poor and vulnerable among the nations, especially where civil unrest has disrupted lives, we pray . . .

That first responders might be protected in their labors to stop and heal suffering, we pray . . .

That all gathered here might recognize signs of distress and sorrow in our loved ones and seek to help them, we pray . . .

Lord God, you free our eyes from tears, our feet from stumbling, and our souls from death. Hear us this day as we seek always to walk with joy in your everlasting mercy. We ask this through Christ our Lord. **Amen.**

TWENTY-FIFTH SUNDAY IN ORDINARY TIME

Prayer

Lord of true riches, you invite us to value what lasts and to labor with faithfulness and humility.

Guide us to act with generosity and to rejoice in your presence so that our lives may witness your abundance and inspire hope in all we meet. **Amen.**

Gospel **Mark 9:30-37**

Jesus and his disciples left from there and began a journey through Galilee, but he did not wish anyone to know about it. He was teaching his disciples and telling them, "The Son of Man is to be handed over to men and they will kill him, and three days after his death the Son of Man will rise." But they did not understand the saying, and they were afraid to question him.

They came to Capernaum and, once inside the house, he began to ask them, "What were you arguing about on the way?" But they remained silent. They had been discussing among themselves on the way who was the greatest. Then he sat down, called the Twelve, and said to them, "If anyone wishes to be first, he shall be the last of all and the servant of all." Taking a child, he placed it in their midst, and putting his arms around it, he said to them, "Whoever receives one child such as this in my name, receives me; and whoever receives me, receives not me but the One who sent me."

Brief Silence

For Reflection

Disorder, wars, conflict, envy, passions: all words from the second reading this Sunday, culminating in the gospel, with the disciples arguing with one another. Where do these troubles come from, and why do they seem so persistent? Imagine if we took to heart the words of Jesus in the gospel, "If anyone wishes to be first, he shall be the last of all and the servant of all." As much as it is thanksgiving, our celebration and reception of the Eucharist is also service, solidarity, and our freedom.

✦ Have you ever found yourself locked into endless competition, which goes nowhere? How does the gospel's challenge help you to change such situations?

Brief Silence

Model Universal Prayer (Prayer of the Faithful)

Turning to the Lord who made heaven and earth, we offer our prayers and our petitions.

Response: Lord, hear our prayer.

For the faithful throughout the world and of every generation: may divisions among us come to an end as we seek to love one another in unity and charity, we pray . . .

For leaders of nations, especially those embroiled by conflict: may powers of destruction be overtaken by peace, we pray . . .

For all suffering from wounds inflicted by pride, hate, and the stripping away of rights: may justice and freedom be found for the oppressed, we pray . . .

For us gathered here today: may we welcome the children in our midst, be they our neighbors' or our own, we pray . . .

Loving God, you have called us through your gospel to possess the glory of your Son, Jesus Christ. Hear our prayers this day as we follow your call to serve one another in faith and charity. We ask this through Christ our Lord. **Amen.**

TWENTY-SIXTH SUNDAY IN ORDINARY TIME

Prayer

Lord of all justice, you see beyond outward appearances and know the truth within us. Help us to live with honesty and integrity and to act with fairness and humility so that our choices may reflect your justice and your mercy in every moment. **Amen.**

Gospel **Mark 9:38-43, 45, 47-48**

At that time, John said to Jesus, "Teacher, we saw someone driving out demons in your name, and we tried to prevent him because he does not follow us." Jesus replied, "Do not prevent him. There is no one who performs a mighty deed in my name who can at the same time speak ill of me. For whoever is not against us is for us. Anyone who gives you a cup of water to drink because you belong to Christ, amen, I say to you, will surely not lose his reward.

"Whoever causes one of these little ones who believe in me to sin, it would be better for him if a great millstone were put around his neck and he were thrown into the sea. If your hand causes you to sin, cut it off. It is better for you to enter into life maimed than with two hands to go into Gehenna, into the unquenchable fire. And if your foot causes you to sin, cut it off. It is better for you to enter into life crippled than with two feet to be thrown into Gehenna. And if your eye causes you to sin, pluck it out. Better for you to enter into the kingdom of God with one eye than with two eyes to be thrown into Gehenna, where 'their worm does not die, and the fire is not quenched.'"

Brief Silence

For Reflection

In today's readings, we hear of people preaching, healing, and leading even without formal authorization. In the gospel, Jesus tells John to let a stranger continue driving out demons in his name, because "whoever is not against us is for us." The church affirms that by baptism, all are priest, prophet, and king. Laypeople lead, teach, and evangelize in many important ways. Imagine what our liturgy could be if it included a broader range of voices—especially those that have been historically silenced or marginalized.

✦ What can you, or your community, do to promote greater justice and peace today, especially for those on the margins?

Brief Silence

Model Universal Prayer (Prayer of the Faithful)

Coming before the Lord who watches always over his people, we offer our prayers and petitions.

Response: Lord, hear our prayer.

That the church throughout the world might grow in faith and vibrancy, especially in those places suffering from secularism and atheism, we pray . . .

That our teachers, mentors, and all who lead young people might be granted wisdom as they pass on their knowledge to others, we pray . . .

That all who are unemployed or underemployed might find steady work with livable wages, we pray . . .

That the faithful gathered here might recognize the gifts of others around them as well as their own, we pray . . .

Lord God, your law is perfect and refreshes the soul. May we become ever more perfect in your law as we strive to follow you. We ask this through Christ our Lord. **Amen.**

TWENTY-SEVENTH SUNDAY IN ORDINARY TIME

Prayer

God of all goodness, call us to produce the fruits of justice and mercy in your kingdom. Strengthen our hearts to respond with faithfulness and courage so that our lives may honor your promise and our patience may bear abundant harvest in our world. **Amen.**

Gospel **Mark 10:2-16 (or Mark 10:2-12)**

The Pharisees approached Jesus and asked, "Is it lawful for a husband to divorce his wife?" They were testing him. He said to them in reply, "What did Moses command you?" They replied, "Moses permitted a husband to write a bill of divorce and dismiss her." But Jesus told them, "Because of the hardness of your hearts he wrote you this commandment. But from the beginning of creation, *God made them male and female. For this reason a man shall leave his father and mother and be joined to his wife, and the two shall become one flesh.* So they are no longer two but one flesh. Therefore what God has joined together, no human being must separate." In the house the disciples again questioned Jesus about this. He said to them, "Whoever divorces his wife and marries another commits adultery against her; and if she divorces her husband and marries another, she commits adultery."

And people were bringing children to him that he might touch them, but the disciples rebuked them. When Jesus saw this he became indignant and said to them, "Let the children come to me; do not prevent them, for the kingdom of God belongs to such as these. Amen, I say to you, whoever does not accept the kingdom of God like a child will not enter it." Then he embraced them and blessed them, placing his hands on them.

Brief Silence

For Reflection

Many long for their children to be touched by Jesus, and he welcomes them, embraces them, saying that the kingdom of God belongs to such as these. Jesus is probably not speaking about children who are pure or simplistic, but rather children who are powerless and rely on their parents for everything—shelter, food, love, and more. So too the kingdom of God belongs to those who rely on God, our adopted Father, for everything. As a loving parent, God always reaches out to embrace us.

✦ How can you learn from the children and childlike that God has put before you today?

Brief Silence

Model Universal Prayer (Prayer of the Faithful)

Coming before the Lord with our prayers and petitions, we offer our hopes for ourselves and all the world.

Response: Lord, hear our prayer.

For the church: may the faithful who have experienced divorce and broken relationships find new life and healing in their lives, we pray . . .

For leaders in our communities and in our nations: may they seek always to protect and advocate for the most vulnerable among us, especially children and our elderly, we pray . . .

For families suffering from estrangement and strained relationships: may the grace of Christ Jesus touch their lives and offer them healing and new hope, we pray . . .

For all of us gathered here: that we may learn to honor those who care for us and cherish those who rely on us, we pray . . .

Loving God, you call little children to come to you. Help us to be like children, trusting in you and relying on your care. We ask this through Christ our Lord. **Amen.**

TWENTY-EIGHTH SUNDAY IN ORDINARY TIME

Prayer

Lord, you show the way to eternal life through the treasures of heaven, help us to surrender what binds us to earthly things and follow you with hearts open to your mercy and love, walking faithfully in your ways and holding fast to your promise of life that never ends. **Amen.**

Gospel **Mark 10:17-30 (or Mark 10:17-27)**

As Jesus was setting out on a journey, a man ran up, knelt down before him, and asked him, "Good teacher, what must I do to inherit eternal life?" Jesus answered him, "Why do you call me good? No one is good but God alone. You know the commandments: *You shall not kill; you shall not commit adultery; you shall not steal; you shall not bear false witness; you shall not defraud; honor your father and your mother.*" He replied and said to him, "Teacher, all of these I have observed from my youth." Jesus, looking at him, loved him and said to him, "You are lacking in one thing. Go, sell what you have, and give to the poor and you will have treasure in heaven; then come, follow me." At that statement his face fell, and he went away sad, for he had many possessions.

Jesus looked around and said to his disciples, "How hard it is for those who have wealth to enter the kingdom of God!" The disciples were amazed at his words. So Jesus again said to them in reply, "Children, how hard it is to enter the kingdom of God! It is easier for a camel to pass through the eye of a needle than for one who is rich to enter the kingdom of God." They were exceedingly astonished and said among themselves, "Then who can be saved?" Jesus looked at them and said, "For human beings it is impossible, but not for God.

All things are possible for God." Peter began to say to him, "We have given up everything and followed you." Jesus said, "Amen, I say to you, there is no one who has given up house or brothers or sisters or mother or father or children or lands for my sake and for the sake of the gospel who will not receive a hundred times more now in this present age: houses and brothers and sisters and mothers and children and lands, with persecutions, and eternal life in the age to come."

Brief Silence

For Reflection

A king asked each of his three sons to completely fill an empty room. The eldest son was minister of war and filled the room with boulders; the second son, minister of finance, filled the room with money. The youngest son lived as a hermit and had only his own prayer. At the end of the test the king said to the youngest son, "Your two brothers tried to fill this room with power, with wealth, and they failed. You filled this room with light. You will be my successor."

✦ What people or expectations are holding you back from following God completely?

Brief Silence

(*continued*)

TWENTY-EIGHTH SUNDAY IN ORDINARY TIME

Model Universal Prayer (Prayer of the Faithful)

Seeking the Lord who teaches us wisdom of heart, we offer our prayers and petitions.

Response: Lord, hear our prayer.

That the church throughout the world might be fed and transformed by a renewed love for reading God's word, we pray . . .

That political leaders may relinquish temptation for power and instead seek the prospering of their peoples, we pray . . .

That women who are denied access to education might be protected and defended in their human flourishing, we pray . . .

That those among us experiencing loss will feel hope in God's mercy and peace, we pray . . .

Lord God, with you, all things are possible. Grant us greater trust in your wisdom so that we might share the joy of your salvation with all the world. We ask this through Christ our Lord. **Amen.**

TWENTY-NINTH SUNDAY IN ORDINARY TIME

Prayer

Teacher of true greatness, you call us to follow the way of your Son, who came to serve and not be served, teach us to set aside pride and ambition, to embrace humility in our hearts, and to offer ourselves in loving service, walking always in your example of selfless love. **Amen.**

Gospel **Mark 10:35-45 (or Mark 10:42-45)**

James and John, the sons of Zebedee, came to Jesus and said to him, "Teacher, we want you to do for us whatever we ask of you." He replied, "What do you wish me to do for you?" They answered him, "Grant that in your glory we may sit one at your right and the other at your left." Jesus said to them, "You do not know what you are asking. Can you drink the cup that I drink or be baptized with the baptism with which I am baptized?" They said to him, "We can." Jesus said to them, "The cup that I drink, you will drink, and with the baptism with which I am baptized, you will be baptized; but to sit at my right or at my left is not mine to give but is for those for whom it has been prepared." When the ten heard this, they became indignant at James and John. Jesus summoned them and said to them, "You know that those who are recognized as rulers over the Gentiles lord it over them, and their great ones make their authority over them felt. But it shall not be so among you. Rather, whoever wishes to be great among you will be your servant; whoever wishes to be first among you will be the slave of all. For the Son of Man did not come to be served but to serve and to give his life as a ransom for many."

Brief Silence

For Reflection

In today's gospel, James and John seek to sit on either side of Christ when he enters into glory. How can they be so unabashed about pursuing exactly the wrong thing? The Christian virtue of temperance can help. The *Catechism of the Catholic Church* quotes St. Augustine: "To live well is nothing other than to love God with all one's heart, with all one's soul and with all one's efforts; from this it comes about that love is kept whole and uncorrupted (through temperance)" (CCC 1809).

✦ Are you ready for the cross, or are you hoping for a kind of human exaltation, like James and John?

Brief Silence

Model Universal Prayer (Prayer of the Faithful)

We come before the Lord in hope and confidence as we bring our prayers for ourselves and all the world.

Response: Lord, hear our prayer.

For all the baptized in churches throughout the world: may the faithful who believe in Christ Jesus grow in confidence in his mercy and in collaboration with one another, we pray . . .

For leaders of our nations and for those running for election: may those seeking positions do so in order to serve their constituents, never to gain power or to secure their own interests, we pray . . .

For all who are suffering in mind, body, and spirit: may they trust in the Lord and find healing in his mercy, we pray . . .

For all gathered here and for our families and friends: may we encourage each other in love and make time to be present for one another, we pray . . .

Lord God, we come to you with confidence in your grace and wonder at the wideness of your mercy. Hear our prayers this day as we offer them for ourselves and for all the world. We ask this through Christ our Lord. **Amen.**

THIRTIETH SUNDAY IN ORDINARY TIME

Prayer

Lord who restores our sight, you hear the cries of those who call upon you in faith, open our eyes to recognize your presence, strengthen our hearts to trust without hesitation, and help us to follow you with courage and joy, walking always in the light of your mercy. **Amen.**

Gospel **Mark 10:46-52**

As Jesus was leaving Jericho with his disciples and a sizable crowd, Bartimaeus, a blind man, the son of Timaeus, sat by the roadside begging. On hearing that it was Jesus of Nazareth, he began to cry out and say, "Jesus, son of David, have pity on me." And many rebuked him, telling him to be silent. But he kept calling out all the more, "Son of David, have pity on me." Jesus stopped and said, "Call him." So they called the blind man, saying to him, "Take courage; get up, Jesus is calling you." He threw aside his cloak, sprang up, and came to Jesus. Jesus said to him in reply, "What do you want me to do for you?" The blind man replied to him, "Master, I want to see." Jesus told him, "Go your way; your faith has saved you." Immediately he received his sight and followed him on the way.

Brief Silence

For Reflection

"Master, I want to see." Often we struggle to see our faith community for who we actually are: the Body of Christ, the full and consciously engaged and active people of God. We can decide for ourselves, in any given context, what manner of speaking the truth might be best received, might best achieve a desired result. Those whose hearts and minds are most in need of change are often also the folks we think might need to be spoken to most forcefully. But remember: sometimes kinder voices are needed.

✦ If Jesus asked you what you wanted from him, what would you say?

Brief Silence

Model Universal Prayer (Prayer of the Faithful)

The Lord gathers all from the ends of the earth and draws them into one. Drawing our hearts together before the Lord, we pray for the needs of the world.

Response: Lord, hear our prayer.

That our Holy Father, Pope N., might encourage all nations to seek unity and peace, rejecting the darkness of war, we pray . . .

That our leaders will advance policies that protect families, offer support to parents, and ensure safety and security for both the young and the old, we pray . . .

That refugees and migrants, especially those with infants and children, find deliverance from their oppressors, we pray . . .

That we might find greater patience and mercy for our own families and the ones we love most, we pray . . .

Lord God, you gather your people from the ends of the world and draw them to yourself. Hear our prayers this day, and may we grow in solidarity and love with all the people of God. We ask this through Christ our Lord. **Amen.**

THIRTY-FIRST SUNDAY IN ORDINARY TIME

Prayer

Lord, you call us to love you with all our heart and to love our neighbor as ourselves, teach us to place your commandments at the center of our lives, to seek your will in all we do, and to live faithfully in the fullness of your love. **Amen.**

Gospel **Mark 12:28b-34**

One of the scribes came to Jesus and asked him, "Which is the first of all the commandments?" Jesus replied, "The first is this: *Hear, O Israel! The Lord our God is Lord alone! You shall love the Lord your God with all your heart, with all your soul, with all your mind, and with all your strength.* The second is this: *You shall love your neighbor as yourself.* There is no other commandment greater than these." The scribe said to him, "Well said, teacher. You are right in saying, 'He is One and there is no other than he.' And 'to love him with all your heart, with all your understanding, with all your strength, and to love your neighbor as yourself' is worth more than all burnt offerings and sacrifices." And when Jesus saw that he answered with understanding, he said to him, "You are not far from the kingdom of God." And no one dared to ask him any more questions.

Brief Silence

For Reflection

Both we and our communities change over time—our needs, experiences, and perspectives shift. These changes should shape how we engage with Scripture and how we prepare for worship. One way to re-engage creatively and prayerfully is through *lectio divina*—a tradition of reading Scripture not just for study but for transformation. This practice can be used by anyone looking to listen more deeply to God's word, alone or in a group, in one sitting or over several days.

✦ Like the scribe, is Jesus challenging you to widen your sense of what it means to love your neighbors, both the ones you know and those you do not know?

Brief Silence

Model Universal Prayer (Prayer of the Faithful)

Coming before the Lord, who is our rock and our redeemer, we offer our prayers and petitions.

Response: Lord, hear our prayer.

For the church: may the faithful of all ages grow in strength of fervor for Christ and in mercy for their neighbors, we pray . . .

For all who serve their countries, their regions, and their cities: may their work be guided by love and respect for their colleagues and their constituents, we pray . . .

For those who have suffered at the hands of their neighbors: may a renewed and right spirit reign, and reconciliation be found, we pray . . .

For all gathered here before the Living One: may we remember always to pray for our loved ones and our enemies, we pray . . .

O God, to love you and to love our neighbor is worth more than all burnt offerings and sacrifices. Hear the prayers which we offer you today for the love of all the world. We ask this through Christ our Lord. **Amen.**

Prayer

Gracious God, you call your people to live in holiness and mercy. Inspire us to follow the path of the saints, to embrace humility, mercy, and righteousness, and to rejoice in your promises, so that one day we may share fully in the joy of your heavenly kingdom. **Amen.**

Gospel **Matt 5:1-12a**

When Jesus saw the crowds, he went up the mountain, and after he had sat down, his disciples came to him. He began to teach them, saying: / "Blessed are the poor in spirit, / for theirs is the Kingdom of heaven. / Blessed are they who mourn, / for they will be comforted. / Blessed are the meek, / for they will inherit the land. / Blessed are they who hunger and thirst for righteousness, / for they will be satisfied. / Blessed are the merciful, / for they will be shown mercy. / Blessed are the clean of heart, / for they will see God. / Blessed are the peacemakers, / for they will be called children of God. / Blessed are they who are persecuted for the sake of righteousness, / for theirs is the Kingdom of heaven. / Blessed are you when they insult you and persecute you and utter every kind of evil against you falsely because of me. Rejoice and be glad, for your reward will be great in heaven."

Brief Silence

For Reflection

Who is the holiest person you know? What is it about them that causes you to see holiness? Call to mind this person's face: their smile, their eyes, their hair . . . Yet if we want to see holiness, we must turn our gaze elsewhere. In the Sermon on the Mount, Jesus tells us to look to the poor in spirit, to the peacemakers, to those who hunger and thirst for righteousness. Seeing people in this way is the closest we will come to seeing the face of God.

✦ Who are those you consider "holy" in your life? How have they affected you?

Brief Silence

Model Universal Prayer (Prayer of the Faithful)

The Lord hears the prayers of his faithful ones. In confidence we pray to the Lord.

Response: Lord, hear our prayer.

For the church: may we rejoice in all the saints, and follow their example as we seek to love and serve the Lord, we pray . . .

For leaders of nations: may they seek wisdom, virtue, and holiness in their daily labors, we pray . . .

For all who are burdened: may they not lose hope, but find confidence and care, we pray . . .

For us gathered here: may we invite the joy of the saints into our daily lives, enriching our families, schools, and workplaces with love for Christ, we pray . . .

O God, you have called us all to be your children in our baptism. Hear our prayers this day and strengthen our resolve to live as your saints did, conforming to the will of your Son, Jesus Christ, our Lord, who lives and reigns with you in the Holy Spirit, God forever and ever. **Amen.**

THE COMMEMORATION OF ALL THE FAITHFUL DEPARTED (ALL SOULS' DAY)

Prayer

Merciful God, our hope and strength, you promise life to all who believe in you. Receive the souls of our departed loved ones into your tender care. Strengthen us in hope and faith, so that one day we may rejoice together in your eternal presence. **Amen.**

Gospel **John 6:37-40 (or other options for All Souls' Day from the Lectionary [L 668] or those given in the Masses for the Dead [nos. 1011–1016])**

Jesus said to the crowds: "Everything that the Father gives me will come to me, and I will not reject anyone who comes to me, because I came down from heaven not to do my own will but the will of the one who sent me. And this is the will of the one who sent me, that I should not lose anything of what he gave me, but that I should raise it on the last day. For this is the will of my Father, that everyone who sees the Son and believes in him may have eternal life, and I shall raise him on the last day."

Brief Silence

For Reflection

We are all familiar with the expression "true colors," when someone lets their "real selves" show through, revealing more of their heart and soul to the community. The liturgy itself has true colors too, which reveal something of the inner character of the celebration or season. For example, black is symbolic of death and mourning and may be used at funeral Masses or the feast of All Souls. Following Vatican II norms, however, white is the preferred color since it reminds us of the resurrection and our baptism.

✦ For whom do you pray this All Souls' Day?

Brief Silence

Model Universal Prayer (Prayer of the Faithful)

The Lord listens to all those who come to him in faith. Let us offer our prayers and petitions.

Response: Lord, hear our prayer.

For the church: may we encourage vocations to the priestly and religious life, and to the permanent diaconate, we pray . . .

For our parents, teachers, and mentors: may those who guide us now, and those who have gone before us, be guided with God's grace, we pray . . .

For families who have lost loved ones: may they rest in confidence that their loved ones rest in the arms of Christ Jesus, we pray . . .

For all gathered here: may we never cease to follow Christ Jesus who shows us the way to eternal life, we pray . . .

Lord God, you have given us the gift of your Son so that we might learn to follow you. Hear our prayers this day, and strengthen our commitment to live as your Son has shown us. We ask this through Christ our Lord. **Amen.**

THIRTY-SECOND SUNDAY IN ORDINARY TIME

Prayer

Generous God, you see the hearts that give with faith and humility, inspire us to offer ourselves freely without counting the cost, to place our trust in your providence, and to live generously in every moment, following the example of those who give with pure love and steadfast devotion. **Amen.**

Gospel **Mark 12:38-44 (or Mark 12:41-44)**

In the course of his teaching Jesus said to the crowds, "Beware of the scribes, who like to go around in long robes and accept greetings in the marketplaces, seats of honor in synagogues, and places of honor at banquets. They devour the houses of widows and, as a pretext, recite lengthy prayers. They will receive a very severe condemnation."

He sat down opposite the treasury and observed how the crowd put money into the treasury. Many rich people put in large sums. A poor widow also came and put in two small coins worth a few cents. Calling his disciples to himself, he said to them, "Amen, I say to you, this poor widow put in more than all the other contributors to the treasury. For they have all contributed from their surplus wealth, but she, from her poverty, has contributed all she had, her whole livelihood."

Brief Silence

For Reflection

Jesus warns the crowds in today's gospel to beware of the scribes who "as a pretext, recite lengthy prayers." Some of us, especially in moments of improvised prayer, tend to ramble on and on because moments of prayer like these lack structure. Here is a pattern you can follow: Name God. Then name something that God has already done for you. Ask or petition God to do something for you. Close your prayer "through Jesus Christ," because he is our connection to God.

✦ As God's child, how can you receive the sacraments with greater love? How can you pass on that love generously this week?

Brief Silence

Model Universal Prayer (Prayer of the Faithful)

Placing our trust in the God who gives life, we offer our prayers and petitions.

Response: Lord, hear our prayer.

For Pope N., and for our bishops, priests, deacons, and lay ministers who serve the church: may they always find food for their faith in their lives of service, we pray . . .

For peoples experiencing upheaval due to climate change: may their leaders be granted wisdom as they seek humanitarian aid and long-term solutions, we pray . . .

For all who lack access to healthy food, especially young children: may their communities work to alleviate their hunger and enable their flourishing, we pray . . .

For all gathered here today: may we find joy in doing small things for the sake of others and for God, we pray . . .

Loving God, you fill the hungry with good things and send the rich away empty. Hear our prayers this day and fill us with the desire to always do your will. We ask this through Christ our Lord. **Amen.**

THIRTY-THIRD SUNDAY IN ORDINARY TIME

Prayer

God whose kingdom draws near, you call us to watch and remain faithful in every season. Keep our hearts attentive to your presence and strengthen our hope in your promises. Help us to live each day in readiness, so that we may greet your coming with joy and unwavering trust in your love. **Amen.**

Gospel **Mark 13:24-32**

Jesus said to his disciples: "In those days after that tribulation the sun will be darkened, and the moon will not give its light, and the stars will be falling from the sky, and the powers in the heavens will be shaken.

"And then they will see 'the Son of Man coming in the clouds' with great power and glory, and then he will send out the angels and gather his elect from the four winds, from the end of the earth to the end of the sky.

"Learn a lesson from the fig tree. When its branch becomes tender and sprouts leaves, you know that summer is near. In the same way, when you see these things happening, know that he is near, at the gates. Amen, I say to you, this generation will not pass away until all these things have taken place. Heaven and earth will pass away, but my words will not pass away.

"But of that day or hour, no one knows, neither the angels in heaven, nor the Son, but only the Father."

Brief Silence

For Reflection

Speaking of the end times, as is typical for mid-November liturgies, Jesus points our attention to the budding fig tree. When its outward appearance changes and its tender branches sprout leaves, one knows what that signifies: summer is near. In the Rite of Baptism, those gathered hear the celebrant speak of the white garment. The dignity and purity the white garment represents is linked to a burning and zealous faith, the light of Christ for all to see. This is how our Scriptures this weekend call us to live.

✦ Are you ready for Christ? Do you believe that he was there before creation and will judge all?

Brief Silence

Model Universal Prayer (Prayer of the Faithful)

Coming before the Lord who reigns over heaven and earth, we offer our petitions as we hope for all the world to be restored to him.

Response: Lord, hear our prayer.

For the faithful scattered throughout the world: may the church grow in strength and mission, especially in places where secularism and apathy reign, we pray . . .

For our politicians, our government officials, and our nation's leaders: may their policies and programs unceasingly promote the dignity of all human beings and care for all creation, we pray . . .

For those burdened with loss, regret, and shame: may the mercy of Christ offer them hope for healing and restoration, we pray . . .

For all gathered together in this place: may we free our hearts from the snares of jealousy and pride, becoming better disciples of Christ, we pray . . .

God our Father, as the days of your Son's coming draw near, draw our hearts closer to you and fill us with the strength to stand before you and rejoice in your presence. We ask this through Christ our Lord. **Amen.**

OUR LORD JESUS CHRIST, KING OF THE UNIVERSE

Prayer

Christ, our King, you reign in justice and mercy, and you come to gather all creation under your loving care. Awaken our hearts and strengthen our faith to follow you without hesitation and lead us joyfully into the fullness of your eternal kingdom. **Amen.**

Gospel **John 18:33b-37**

Pilate said to Jesus, "Are you the King of the Jews?" Jesus answered, "Do you say this on your own or have others told you about me?" Pilate answered, "I am not a Jew, am I? Your own nation and the chief priests handed you over to me. What have you done?" Jesus answered, "My kingdom does not belong to this world. If my kingdom did belong to this world, my attendants would be fighting to keep me from being handed over to the Jews. But as it is, my kingdom is not here." So Pilate said to him, "Then you are a king?" Jesus answered, "You say I am a king. For this I was born and for this I came into the world, to testify to the truth. Everyone who belongs to the truth listens to my voice."

Brief Silence

For Reflection

We belong only to Christ, who is eternal. Our identity is far greater than any world leader can bestow, and our lives are owed to Christ alone. It is his kingdom we strive to build, his peace we work to bring. No matter who wins any election, we all have work to do. In our liturgies and in the world, we must strive—in the words attributed to a few different saints—to pray as if it all depends on God, and act as if it all depends on us.

✦ Are you distracted by power, politics, or turbulence in your life? Why so?

Brief Silence

Model Universal Prayer (Prayer of the Faithful)

Coming before the Lord who reigns over heaven and earth, we offer our prayers for ourselves and all the world.

Response: Lord, hear our prayer.

For the faithful throughout the church: may we live truly as Jesus's disciples, serving in charity and truth and defending the poor and lowly, we pray . . .

For all nations: may the rights of all peoples be protected, respected, and valued, we pray . . .

For people throughout the world who have had their freedoms removed: may their dignity be restored, we pray . . .

For all of us gathered today: may we refuse to become addicted to technology, social media, and self-focused practices that attempt to rule our lives, we pray . . .

Lord God, your dominion is an everlasting dominion that will never be taken away. May all the world come to know you, who alone reigns for ever and ever. We ask this through Christ our Lord. **Amen.**

CONTRIBUTORS

Martin Erspamer, OSB, is a monk and a hermit of Saint Meinrad Archabbey in southern Indiana. He is a well-known liturgical artist and liturgical consultant. Erspamer works in a wide range of media, including pottery, stained glass, and wood, and is nationally known for his illustration of sacred themes.

Katharine E. Harmon is a pastoral liturgist and American Catholic historian serving as the project director for the Obsculta Preaching Initiative at Saint John's School of Theology and Seminary in Collegeville, Minnesota. A graduate of the University of Notre Dame's liturgical studies program, Harmon has contributed both scholarly and pastoral pieces on topics of liturgical renewal and American Catholic faith and practice, including *There Were Also Many Women There: Lay Women in the Liturgical Movement in the United States, 1926–59* (Liturgical Press, 2013) and the award-winning *Mary and the Liturgical Year: A Pastoral Resource* (Liturgy Training Publications, 2023). She has served as a church musician for more than 25 years, and resides in St. Joseph, Minnesota, with her husband and two children.

Orin E. Johnson has held professional music and liturgy positions for 25 years, currently at St. Margaret of Scotland Catholic Church in St. Louis, Missouri. He holds degrees in music and theology from Harvard University, Radford University, and Aquinas Institute of Theology. His liturgical music is published with OCP and GIA; he is the author of *Incarnate in Word and Song: Exploring Music in Liturgy and Life* (Liturgical Press, 2023), and has other writings published by Liturgical Press, Liguori, and Twenty-Third Publications. He is active nationally as a speaker, performer, catechist, and retreat and workshop leader.

Rámond Mitchell serves as director of liturgy for Our Lady of Grace Church and School in Edina, Minnesota. Previously he served as assistant director of liturgy at the Basilica of Saint Mary in Minneapolis, and parish liturgist and then as director of liturgy at Saint George-in-the-East Church in London, UK. Originally from the Bahamas, he earned a bachelor of arts in theology from Saint John's University (Collegeville, Minnesota) and a master of arts in theology and ministry from Boston College. He has been a dedicated cantor and psalmist at Westminster Cathedral in London and enjoys music making and cooking outside of his professional work.

Matthew Sherman serves as the director of lifelong learning and educational effectiveness at Saint John's School of Theology and Seminary in Collegeville, Minnesota. His writing and teaching involve the intersection of theology and ministry, the role of ethics in historical theology, and connections between sacramental and moral thought. He teaches courses in fundamental morals, historical theology, bioethics, marriage and family, and Catholic social teaching.